happy belly
GELATO

FINDING ITALY'S BEST GELATERIAS

FANCY
PANTS
PRESS

Series Editor
Michael McGarry

Brand Identity and Book Design
ALUSIV, INC. | Philadelphia, PA | www.alusiv.com
Richard Cress, Ned Drew, Sandy Knight,
Brenda MacManus, Jessie Taing, Mark Wills

Photography
Richard Cress, Charles Whitney, Rachel McGarry, Michael McGarry

Production Consultant
Jim Bindas, BOOK PRODUCTIONS LLC

Copy Editor
Sharon Parker

Our thanks to John and Stephanie Reitano of CAPOGIRO GELATO ARTISANS,
Philadelphia, PA for graciously participating in this effort as a knowledgable
resource and "product model" for some of the photographs in this book.

Fancy Pants Press, Happy Belly, and their corresponding logos are trademarks
of Fancy Pants Press.

Printed in China.

Library of Congress Control Number: 2004090723
ISBN 0-9749118-0-1

Bulk purchases are available to gelaterias, ice cream parlors, institutions,
corporations, organizations, charities, and individuals at special discounts.
For more information please visit our website.

Published by
Fancy Pants Press
2739 Irving Avenue South
Minneapolis, MN 55408
612.872.2382
info@happybellyguides.com
www.happybellyguides.com

FANCY
PANTS
PRESS

10 9 8 7 6 5 4 3 2 1

The Happy Belly Guide series is committed to bringing a smile to every reader's tummy. There are plenty of great books that will lead you to the best restaurants around the globe — with endless pages describing three-course meals, wine lists, and expensive decors. While we love such places, our books cover the other side of the food spectrum — the shops, shacks, and parlors that specialize in the creation of decadent, mouth-watering delicacies. Health consciousness be damned, this is the food you rightfully crave, food that will always make your belly happy.

How to use this Guide

The purpose of this guide is to help readers find and eat the best gelato in Italy. The layout is intuitive, with sections divided alphabetically by region, then by city, and finally by gelateria. At the end you'll find a glossary of selected Italian words and a separate glossary of flavors.

We realize that navigating through foreign cities is confusing and for that reason have included addresses, directions from major monuments and sites, and, for larger cities, illustrated maps.

We have painstakingly attempted to include accurate operating hours, but please keep in mind that hours frequently fluctuate from week to week and shops may close for months at a time without any notice. Phone numbers, which also have a tendency to change, are listed where possible, so please feel free to call in advance.

Each gelateria in this guide is a worthwhile destination, but some have features that deserve special recognition:

🅑 *Shops whose gelato ranks as the best of the best.*

🌅 *Locales that have an ambiance, setting, or scene that should not be missed.*

🪑 *Locales that offer waiter service and/or comfortable outdoor seating.*

In addition to the entries, throughout the guide you will find special sections under the headings TIPS & INFO and GELATO LORE.

TIPS & INFO provide hints, advice, and facts that are meant to enhance any gelato experience. GELATO LORE sections give readers the background on the history and myths surrounding this long-revered treat.

Finally, although we stand by all of the selected entries, we realize that a few good shops may have slipped our attention. If you stumble across a great gelateria that you think merits mention in future editions or want to comment on any of the entries please feel free to send us an e-mail at **info@happybellyguides.com** or post a review at **www.happybellyguides.com**.

ACKNOWLEDGEMENTS

My belly and I would like to thank everyone who helped make this book a reality, including

Guido Reni, the Baroque master who prompted this endeavor;

Lucrezia, Stephania, and the staff at Cultura Italiana Bologna, who taught me how to say "three scoops" (*tre gusti*) in Italian;

Todd and Lisa McDonald, traveling companions and lovers of lardo;

Julia Smyth-Pinney, for providing comfort, Borromini tours, and great barbecue in a foreign land;

Carola Vannini, who opened up her Roman world and without whose help this book would not have been completed;

Perry Del Ghingaro, for helping me set up shop in Minneapolis;

Teddy Kordonowy, researcher extraordinaire;

Andy Steiner, for her advice and editorial direction;

Steve Couture, who despite breaking both hands in a piñata incident contributed significantly to the development of this book;

La Regina, my rock and a traveler who is always up for a new adventure;

Papa McGarry, who passed down his love of ice cream and whose enthusiasm I try to emulate;

Jan Kordonowy, a whirlwind of creative energy;

Tom Kordonowy, always generous and who after a visit to Testaccio has now eaten every part of a pig;

Sarah and Mike Connelly, whose time at metric camp continues to pay dividends;

Catherine McGarry, who better have a mint chocolate chip ice cream wedding cake;

Oliver Prichard, Bill Meeks, Joey "Jelly Roll" Bartolomeo, Douglas and Maritza Kully, Rebecca Bassin, Lyle Johnson, C.D. Dickerson, Dan Fox, Betsy and Mary Vilett, and Thommy "Freemason" Kordonowy, friends and visitors who helped me tour the country in search of the perfect cone;

Austin, Anna, and Lydia, happy bellies of the future;

and Ray, la mia principessa and daily inspiration.

MENU

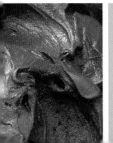

CITY SECTIONS:

OTHER SECTIONS:

BIRTH OF THE BELLY

Italy is a place to enrich your soul and fill your stomach: for every breathtaking Michelangelo and Caravaggio there is a mouthwatering *risotto* and *formaggio*. Travelers read up on *duomos* and *piazzas* but return raving about *mozzarella di bufala* and *spaghetti carbonara*. No different, I, on my first trip to Italy, was excited to visit the Piazza San Marco, the Vatican, and the Bay of Naples only to find myself counting the minutes until my next opportunity to devour more pasta, pizza and prosciutto.

Postcards quickly progressed from descriptions of fountains and vistas into detailed accounts of meals, eventually becoming a running food journal. A conspicuous omission from this correspondence was gelato. I had tried and enjoyed several flavors but had literally not tasted anything to write home about. It was not until the last night of the trip that I had my epiphany, an experience that has had me **eating, dreaming, and living gelato ever since.**

My wife (then girlfriend) and I were lucky enough to happen upon a secluded Roman *trattoria* that fulfilled the fantasy of all travelers: no other tourists and plenty of local charm. We were seated next to a friendly older couple who took it upon themselves to order an entire meal for us before departing. Excited that good food was on the way we hardly noticed the arrival of our new table companions, the extremely hip Fabio and Maddalena.

As the night progressed and our courses, including the classic *carciofi alla romana* (Roman style artichokes) and a savory *abbacchio al forno* (roast suckling lamb), arrived, our neighbors began to take an interest in us. Maddalena broke the silence by complimenting us for ordering authentic local cuisine, not knowing that we had received help. Fabio then asked us how we had found the restaurant and if we knew someone who worked there. Sensing a little suspicion, I told him that we had just stumbled across the place while looking for another restaurant (a lie; we had found it in a guidebook) and joked that the owner had taken pity on us for wearing clothes that had been out of fashion in Italy for three years (probably true).

Falsely assured that his favorite little trattoria was not soon to be overwhelmed by tourists, Fabio opened up. Behind the Gucci, Fabio and Maddalena were just as kind as the other Italians we had met on the trip and for the next hour or so we had a great time talking about our travels and their upcoming visit to the United States. Enjoying our first chance to interact with members of the

Italian glitterati, I failed to foresee the dangerous significance of the fast-approaching waiter. As he asked what we would like for dessert, I froze with panic, thinking that we would blow our cover by ordering something not authentic. My wife, always two steps ahead, asked our new-found friends what they would recommend. After a brief pause in which their surprise turned into astonishment, Maddalena informed us that no one orders dessert in this neighborhood, everyone goes to Giolitti instead. Reading our confused faces, Fabio offered to take us there personally, and before I could say *cioccolato*, we found ourselves in the back seat of his Alfa Romeo.

Having negotiated several winding streets that resembled pedestrian walkways, we triple-parked the car and began walking toward a loud clamor. As we turned a corner, the illuminated Giolitti sign came into view — a must-see sight second only to the nearby Pantheon. Underneath this beacon swarmed what seemed to be the entire Roman populace, either fighting to get in or exiting with a cone in hand.

After wedging indoors, I viewed the interior for the first time and was struck by both the size and diversity of the crowd. In addition to the regular Italian clientele, the shop was packed by a rainbow of customers, resembling a gelato United Nations. All the stereotypical tourists were there: the Japanese man taking a photo of the cashier, the sunburned Brit, the sweet-toothed German woman eating a six-scoop cone, and a gaggle of sub-five-foot Malaysian nuns.

Playing the role of the clueless American, I made a beeline for the counter only to be grabbed by Fabio and told that we had to pay the cashier first. Realizing that there was no way to play this one cool, I followed him to the cashier and awaited the cold shoulder treatment. Instead, Fabio seemed more excited then ever, telling me about the history of the place and what flavors I should try. After paying, we made our way to the back of the seven-deep crowd around the counter and together jockeyed our way into ordering position. As my time came I stood my ground and asked for **pistacchio** and **fragola** (strawberry), a conservative but solid choice, although at the time I thought it was an exotic mixture. As I backed my way out of the crowd I took my first bite and in a state of sheer pleasure stood momentarily paralyzed in the center of the room. Never before had I tasted such intense flavors, flavors that seemed to deliver the very essence of their ingredients.

I was awoken from my gelato stupor by my wife tugging me out onto the street. Strolling through the beautiful Roman night I asked Fabio why he enjoyed sharing his favorite gelateria with me, not to mention the hordes of other tourists, after being wary of foreigners at the trattoria. His answer was simple yet eloquent, **"gelato is for everyone."** As we reached the car and said farewell to our newfound gelato guardian angels, I pondered his answer. Replaying our trip I remembered being awestruck by various sites, eating some of the best food I had ever tasted, and falling in love with the Italian way of life, but it was only at the gelateria that I felt as though I had experienced an authentic Italian moment.

Years after this first gelato experience I have come to appreciate the role of the gelateria in modern-day Italy. For centuries, the Italian peninsula has been besieged by foreigners ranging from Greek colonists and Northern barbarians to today's honeymooners and tour groups. While reasons for arrival vary, each group has done its part to disrupt the seemingly idyllic lives of the peninsula's inhabitants. Over time the Italians have constructed subtle barriers to separate themselves from the invading masses, perfecting the process of giving just enough to keep people coming back for more while still maintaining their private lives. Contemporary Italians generally live outside major city centers, frequent local restaurants that are rarely included in guidebooks, and vacation at lesser known, but just as beautiful, locations. As a result, most tourists visiting ancient sites, museums, churches, and fabled coastlines have little contact with Italians outside of the service industries.

Gelaterias, however, are different. Granted there are many shops situated near major sites and train stations that serve sub-par gelato and cater solely to foreigners; but it is also true that **a city's best gelaterias are often in the midst of tourist-friendly zones.** Italians will not settle for anything but the highest quality gelato and not even an aversion to fanny packs and jorts (jean shorts) will stop them from eating at their favorite gelateria regularly. Their discerning taste buds force them to mingle with the occupying masses and have created a class of gelaterias that are unique in their role as Italian melting pots.

There are no better places than these premier sites to enjoy a local delicacy in the company of actual locals.

As an Italophile and gelato fanatic, **I decided to track down these elite gelaterias.** After performing extensive research and surveying a network of expatriates, seasoned travelers, and indispensable Italian friends for advice and suggestions, I compiled a list of over a hundred good gelaterias in the major cities north of and including Naples (a second book covering the South and the islands, especially Sicily, is in the works). Over the past year I visited these shops, refining my palate while expanding my belly as I paired down the list to the following great selections. Some entries, like GIOLITTI, are well-known to both tourists and Italians alike, while others are frequented by locals and only the savviest of visitors. Each of the chosen shops is special in its own way, be it because of location, ambiance, or just exceptional gelato. I hope you find them to be as extraordinary as I did and wish you all the luck in having your own authentic gelato experiences.

find your happy belly...

GELATO BASICS

Compared to negotiating with a Venetian glass merchant or trying to send a package through the Italian post office, ordering gelato is a relatively pleasant experience. Still, there are two basic procedures that will make your experience smoother.

FIRST, it is common practice when visiting a gelateria to **pay the cashier first**, then present your receipt to the server before placing an order. This rule is enforced at all of the larger gelaterias, where servers will not even look your way at peak times unless you have a receipt in hand. At smaller locations, where only one person is working both the counter and register, you can usually order before paying. Regardless of payment etiquette, you will always be served faster if a small tip (about ten cents) has been placed on top of your receipt.

THE SECOND RULE pertains to Italy's arcane tax-paying system (don't ask). When you make a purchase, regardless if it is a small-sized cone or pair of leather stilettos, **you must always leave with a receipt**. Tossing a receipt in a shop's trash can is a good way to get a nasty look, and a *gelataio* (server) may chase you down the street if you leave it on the counter, an awkward experience you want to avoid.

IN ADDITION to adhering to these procedures, there are several other tips that can enhance your overall gelato experience. The art of ordering gelato begins with dealing with gelateria crowds. Many travelers are put off by long lines and end up settling for a lesser cone at an inferior establishment. However, **long lines often mean good gelato** and by embracing the chaos one is usually well-rewarded. Rather than getting frustrated when a few older Italian women or young children cut to the front, use the extra time as an opportunity to survey the flavors and search for any unusual items that may be offered. Pay particular attention to what the Italians are ordering — this can often alert you to a shop's specialty. Many of the best gelaterias produce an ever-changing menu of flavors in order to best utilize certain **seasonal ingredients.** These flavors are often served only a few weeks a year and are among the freshest and tastiest choices you can make. When in doubt ask a server about their *specialità,* most likely, unless they are extremely busy, they will be more than willing to give advice and free samples.

I know that flavor preference is highly personal, but nonetheless I suggest straying from your rotation of favorites every now and again. Each Italian region, city, and for that matter gelateria is unique and by branching out you may find an array of delicious new flavor options. With each order you are given an opportunity to have both a favorite and a new selection, for **it is common practice to order two or three different flavors per cone.** Gelato snobs recommend having two flavors and

never adding toppings, believing that one's palate can be overwhelmed by excess. While I agree that two flavors produce a better overall effect than three, I also think that to each their own, and if someone feels like buying an eight-scoop cone topped with whipped cream and nuts, more power to them.

There is no wrong time to eat gelato, but there are certain times when gelaterias are more fun to visit. Most gelaterias open around noon in order to cater to the after-lunch crowd. A good shop will have a steady stream of customers throughout the day, slowly building to the evening *passeggiata* (stroll) period. During this time Italians flock to the streets, running errands, meeting friends, window shopping, and eating gelato. Around the better gelaterias at this time it seems as though every other person within a three-block radius is walking with a cone in hand. After seven o'clock things die down a little until people begin to file out of dinner. Starting at 8:00 P.M., a gelateria begins to experience an influx of customers starting with Japanese, followed by Americans, Northern Europeans, and ending in a crescendo of Spaniards and Italians. Between 10:00 P.M. and 12:00 A.M. any gelateria worth a lick is packed full of customers during high-travel season. Typically, most shops close around midnight, but on the weekends some gelaterias stay open until the early morning and rival neighboring bars and clubs for the title of place to be.

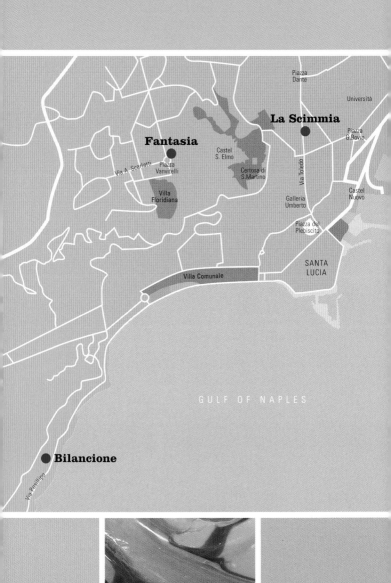

La Scimmia

Fantasia

Bilancione

Piazza Dante

Università

Piazza G. Bovio

Via Toledo

Castel S. Elmo

Castel Nuovo

Certosa di S. Martino

Galleria Umberto

Via A. Scarlatti

Piazza Vanvitelli

Piazza del Plebiscito

Villa Floridiana

SANTA LUCIA

Villa Comunale

GULF OF NAPLES

Via Posillipo

NAPLES

Despite its lawless nature and general aura of chaos, Naples maintains an irresistible old-world charm. For every pickpocket who acts as if it is your duty to give up your wallet, there is a *nonna* (grandmother) on a corner selling freshly baked goods or a family-run pizzeria hidden on a back street. It is not uncommon for visitors to form a love/hate relationship with the city, alternating between overwhelming feelings of fear and exhaustion, and longing to drop everything and settle within its confines.

Gelatowise I found that only the strong survive. While the following entries are more than worthy of this guide, there is a dearth of competitors for a town this size. Down along the coast on the Riviera di Chiáia there is a series of grand old cafés that serve gelato, but I found that while the setting was beautiful, the gelato was not exceptional. Filling the void is a multitude of shaved-ice stands, allowing frazzled travelers the opportunity to buy refreshing treats from old pushcarts throughout town.

Bilancione

ADDRESS Via Posillipo 238
PHONE 081 7691923
HOURS 7a–12a, closed Mon
DIRECTIONS *Southwest of the city center in the Posillipo district, facing the bay.*

Media mogul and Italian Prime Minister Silvio Berlusconi's nearby house has beautiful views and easy access to the sea, but it is rumored that the real reason he chose this affluent neighborhood was to be close enough to walk to BILANCIONE. After visiting this shop, I cannot say that I blame him. Despite its nondescript façade, and a location outside the city center, BILANCIONE has instant name recognition among Neapolitans. The reasons for this are twofold: picturesque views of Vesuvius, Sorrento and Capri, and unforgettable gelato. The shop's **nocciola** (hazelnut) is a nutty delight and the Sicilian-inspired **cassata**, with chunks of candied fruit, is delicious. I recommend taking a cab or bus to the shop, always a memorable experience in Naples, and descending back into town with cone in hand along the elevated road overlooking the sea.

Fantasia 🐾

ADDRESS Piazza Vanvitelli 22
PHONE 081 5788383
HOURS 7a–12a daily
DIRECTIONS *In the Vomero district, a ten-minute walk west from the Certosa and Castel S. Elmo.*

With three locations scattered throughout town (the other two are located at *Via Toledo 381* and *Via Cilea 80)*, FANTASIA has become synonymous with gelato in Naples. Of the three, I particularly enjoyed the *Vanvitelli* location, situated high above the city in the heart of the upper-middle-class neighborhood of Vomero. FANTASIA'S outdoor seating area is the perfect place to rest and treat yourself after a day of negotiating funiculars, vista gazing, and sightseeing at the nearby Certosa and Castel S. Elmo. If you have the energy, another option is to get your cone to go and stroll through the nearby Villa Floridiana, one of Naples' nicest parks. The gelato here lives up to its name, with a fantastical selection including **cioccolato con limoncello**, chocolate with a lemon-based liqueur, **benevento**, a white chocolate medley, and a delicious **banana** gelato layered with sliced fresh fruit.

La Scimmia 🐵

ADDRESS Piazza Carità 4
PHONE 081 5520272
HOURS 10a–12a daily
DIRECTIONS *On the west side of Piazza Carità facing Via Toledo.*

After a day of dodging *ragazzi* on *motorini* (scooters) while navigating through the city's warren of narrow clothes-lined streets, you may find yourself comparing Naples to an urban jungle. It is only fitting then that in the heart of the old city LA SCIMMIA (the monkey) reigns supreme. Situated in the bustling Piazza Carità, this local institution has served generations of Neapolitans since its opening in 1933. Ask anyone in town and they will be able to tell you where to find the monkey — and more than likely will warmly continue talking until you have found out which flavors they think are best, how old they were the first time they ate there, and why Neapolitan food is superior to northern cuisine. Surprisingly, there really is a monkey in the form of a statuette perched above the entranceway greeting all as they walk in. The house specialties are the **torrone**, a nougat concoction, **stracciatella** (chocolate chip), and **fior di latte azzurri**, an electric blue version of the Italian classic. There is also another shop closer to the water at *Piazza Trieste e Trento 54.*

GELATO LORE

Ice Age

Gelato as we know it is a relatively new delicacy, but use of ice and snow for gastronomic purposes is an ancient practice that has been passed on from civilization to civilization. Records of this practice were first recorded in the cuneiform tablets of the Mesopotamians, which reveal how wealthy citizens would use ice brought in from far-off locales to cool their drinks. During the next three millennia, recipes and chilling techniques slowly spread throughout the Middle East, eventually making their way to the Greek empire. Here ice and snow were stored in all major cities and, in true democratic spirit, were used to chill drinks by not only the elite, but by soldiers and everyday citizens as well.

By the time of the Roman Empire, chilled drink techniques had evolved to a culinary art, reaching a pinnacle during the reign of Nero Claudius (A.D. 37–68). In preparation for his lavish banquets, Nero would command the swiftest runners in the land to bring snow from distant mountain peaks to the storage pits on his palace grounds. As the parties began, the snow would be packed into the outer chamber of a newly designed glass in order to chill the wines and fruit juices held in the inner chamber. This two-chambered glass had the two-fold benefit of eliminating any watery dilution and preventing any mixing of the beverages with much traveled and oft dirty snow. The end result was a *granita*-like concoction so prized that only the emperor could determine who was worthy of a serving. Alas, like so many of Rome's ancient treasures, the practice of chilling drinks vanished from the peninsula as the Western empire crumbled, and would not be in vogue again for centuries.

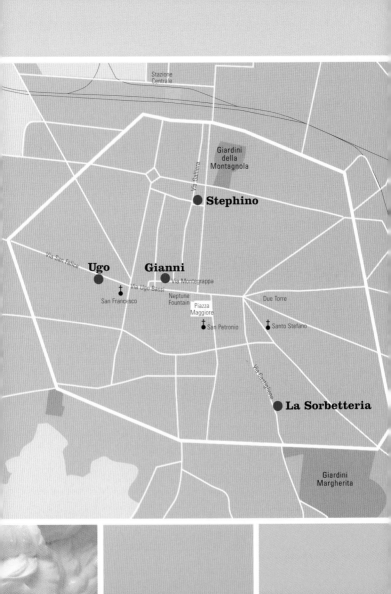

BOLOGNA is a town that takes its

food seriously. Nicknamed *la grassa* (the fat), the city's cuisine, from the delicious *tagliatelle al ragù* (the inspiration for the world-renowned spaghetti Bolognese) to the heart-stopping *lasagne verdi* (green lasagna), will add a few pounds to even the most health-conscious of travelers.

The town's gelaterias proudly uphold this culinary tradition, providing the best selection of shops outside of Rome. While the following entries are indeed the best in town, there are a number of gelaterias not listed — COMMERCIANTI and GELATERIA DELLE MOLINE to name two — that would be gastronomical landmarks in other cities. Gelato-seeking visitors should memorize the word **cestino,** which means "trash can" in other towns, but in Bologna is the term for the ubiquitous flat-bottomed cones. A word to the wise, bring loose-fitting pants, before you know it Bologna will cause your belly to grow a belly of its own.

Gianni

ADDRESS   Via Montegrappa 11/a
PHONE   051 233008
HOURS   Mon, Tue, Thu–Sat 12p–1a, Sun 11a–1a, closed Wed
DIRECTIONS   *From the Neptune fountain, walk west on Via Ugo Bassi, take a right on Via Calcavinazzi, and take first left onto Via Montegrappa. The shop is on the corner of Via Montegrappa and Via degli Usberti.*

GIANNI is the best gelateria within five minutes of Piazza Maggiore and for that reason is one of the most

frequented spots in town. During the day and into the early evening the shop is busy serving locals, businessmen and women, and couples toting *bambini,* but it is not until later on that it really begins to buzz. On hot summer nights, the line of hip Italians in front of GIANNI seems more like a crowd waiting to get into a new nightclub or fashion show than what you'd expect at a gelateria. Prada shoes, Gucci bags, and Armani jeans all vie for space at the long counter. Despite the see-and-be-seen atmosphere, it is the award-winning gelato that attracts this stylish clientele. Although the classic choices are good, you should really go out on a limb here and try one of the many unusual flavors that have made GIANNI famous. The **frutti dimenticati** (forgotten fruit) are particularly interesting, featuring **corniola** (cornel berry) and **nespola giapponese** (Japanese medlar). True daredevils should try either the **inferno** or the **purgatorio**, flavors whose ingredients are best left to the imagination.

La Sorbetteria (Castiglione) ₿ ☀

ADDRESS Via Castiglione 44

PHONE 051 233257

HOURS 8a–11:45p, closed Tue, abbreviated hours in August

DIRECTIONS *From the Two Towers walk south on Via Castiglione. The shop is on the east side of the street between Via Castellata and Via Rialto.*

A fifteen-minute walk from the Due Torre down one of the most charming streets in Bologna, LA SORBETTERIA is a must for any gelato lover. Of all the gelaterias I visited for this book, this shop ranks as one of my favorites. The shining coverlets, the immaculate gelato machines proudly displayed for all to see, and the apron-clad matrons calmly serving behind the counter all point to the love and care that is put into the production of each flavor. The shop uses the freshly made chocolate from a neighboring chocolate shop to produce a variety of flavors, including a to-die-for **cioccolato** (chocolate) and a chunky **stracciatella**. Although these flavors are superb, the real reason locals line up out the door during spring and summer evenings is for a taste of **Michelangelo**, **Ludovico**, or **Eduardo**. These house specialties combine almonds, caramel, chocolate, hazelnuts and other fresh ingredients in such a way that will inspire you to return again and again in the hope of discovering yet another subtle taste within their creamy texture.

Stephino

ADDRESS Via Galliera 49/b

PHONE 051 246736

HOURS 1p–1a, closed Mon

DIRECTIONS *From the Neptune fountain walk north on Via dell' Indipendenza for about 10 minutes, take a left onto Via S. Giuseppe, and take the first right onto Via Galliera. The shop is on the east side of the street across from Via Strazzacappe.*

STEPHINO takes full advantage of the famed Bolognese porticoes by having customers wait outside while ordering from its tiny street-side counter. Thanks to the spillover of the crowd from the neighboring bar/café there is always a lively nighttime atmosphere. The shop makes very good gelato, including the **Mediterraneo** (pistachio with almonds and pine nuts) and the **Cuneo** (chocolate and rum). The real reason to visit STEPHINO, however, is for its **granita**. A Sicilian delicacy, granita is basically a flavored ice slushy occasionally placed between layers of fresh whipped cream. Those from the island as well as Southern Italians have been known to gripe that their Northern brethren focus only on gelato and subsequently cannot produce a decent granita. This is not the case at STEPHINO, where granita comes first, drawing transplanted Sicilians and Southerners longing for a taste of home. The **cioccolato** is not to be missed and the **fragola** evokes the essence of strawberry shortcake.

Ugo 🝔

ADDRESS   Via San Felice 24

PHONE   051 263849

HOURS   Sun 11:30a–1:15p and 3:30p–10p, Wed–Sat 3:30p–11p,
          closed Mon and Tue, most of August

DIRECTIONS   *From the Neptune fountain walk west on Via Ugo Bassi until it turns*
            into Via San Felice. The shop is on the south side of the street
            between Via del Borghetto and Via Paradiso.

If you are in Bologna long enough
you will hear of the legendary UGO.
It will start with whispers about the
creamiest **pistacchio** in town and
slowly build until you've heard all
you can about sinful **cioccolato** and
thirst-quenching **limone** (lemon).
When you finally crack and begin
asking locals where you can find
this gelato paradise, they will tell

you that the question is not where but when. UGO is on
one of the city's main streets in the western part of town,
so finding it is no problem; finding it open is the trouble.
Countless times customers arrive at the shop only to find
the steel grate pulled down, either due to its limited
weekly schedule or because it has closed for one of its
many holidays. The fact that servings are half that of
normal portions completes UGO's forbidden-fruit aura.
The uninitiated are left to ask whether a trip to UGO is
worth the trouble, but tasting their gelato just once will
convert even the most frustrated of customers, proving
that the reputation is more than justified. This is a place to
enjoy the basics, from the aforementioned staples to their
exceptional **crema** (custard/French vanilla) and **fragola**.

MODENA

Surprisingly there is not a stand-out gelateria in this town of refined tastes, home to Ferraris, mink-wearing bicyclists, and Pavarotti. The town does, however, produce the best gelato topping in all of Italy — **balsamic vinegar.**

In Modena, balsamic is a religion, with a selection available at seemingly every store that ranges from the mass-produced to those made and bottled by the man standing across the counter. The gourmet versions are aged from ten to forty years and are priced higher as they get older. For gelato purposes, I believe the more aged the better, as the process both thickens and fortifies the vinegar over time. With just a few drops of forty-year balsamic, a scoop of vanilla gelato turns into a flavorful treat, similar to a hot fudge sundae, but with a tangy kick.

Many of the town's restaurants offer this as a dessert (my favorite is DA DANILO, *Via Coltellini 31*) and I suggest buying a bottle to replicate their efforts and astound dinner guests back home. While there is great debate as to which balsamic is best, I purchase my balsamic from stand sixty-three in the covered market. The Famiglia Bertani brand is as good as I've ever had and you always get a chance to talk to a member of the Bertani family when purchasing.

For those who want gelato sans balsamic try GELATERIA DUCALE *(Piazza Roma 4 & Via Albinelli 52)* or GELATERIA K2 *(Corso Canal Grande 67)*.

TIPS & INFO

The Difference between Ice Cream and Gelato

There is a common misconception that ice cream and gelato are one and the same. While it is true that the direct translation for ice cream is *gelato* and both come in a variety of flavors that can be served in a cone, there exist subtle differences that in aggregate create distinct delicacies.

As its name suggests, ice cream is made with fresh cream, producing a butterfat content in the range of 10 percent to 30 percent. **Gelato, on the other hand, is usually made with milk, water, or soy** as a base and maintains a fat content between 0 percent and 10 percent. The effect is more than just the obvious advantage that gelato is a healthier alternative. Cream saturates taste buds, causing its richness to prevail over other flavors and making ice cream preferable for those who favor sweetness above all else. Conversely, gelato emphasizes nondairy ingredients, with the less fatty bases providing a subtler background and allowing for individual flavors to dominate the palate.

The use of cream versus milk, water, and soy suggests that ice cream would be a more condensed, richer treat; however, this is not the case. Gelato is able to hold its own in this regard due to a disparity in the amount of overrun, which is the percentage of air that is beaten and blown into batches of ice cream during mixing and freezing processes. A significant amount of overrun is necessary in ice cream, because without air the cream-based mixtures would be rock hard and unservable; however, too much overrun leads to a fast-dripping, unfulfilling scoop. The best premium ice creams have an overrun level of about 50 percent (meaning that 25 percent of the product is air), whereas mass-produced brands, seeking to maximize profit margins, run as high as 100 percent. On average, gelato has less than 30 percent overrun, containing only the amount that is naturally incorporated during the churning process.

Good gelato exists in a semifrozen state in which it is firm but not hard, appearing as though it will begin dripping soon but never actually getting to that point. Since gelato includes less air, each batch is more concentrated, leading to a more intense taste.

Collectively, these differences produce three unique products:

1   MASS-PRODUCED ICE CREAM, with high overrun and mid-range butterfat content, is airy and generally has a muted taste.

2   PREMIUM ICE CREAM, with medium overrun and high butterfat content, is sweet and very creamy.

3   GELATO, with low overrun and low butterfat content, is the healthiest, densest, and most flavorful of the three.

PARMA

Although it contains a beautiful Duomo and Baptistery, charming streets, and exceptional art collections, Parma will always be thought of first and foremost as a culinary magnet. Throughout the year Italians and other gastronomical travelers flock to the town for a taste of Parma's namesake cheese and ham as well as other local delicacies.

Gelateria la Pilotta

ADDRESS	Strada Garibaldi Giuseppe 29/b
PHONE	0521 206406
HOURS	11a–12a, closed Tue
DIRECTIONS	*On the east side of the Piazza del Pace facing the Palazzo della Pilotta (home of the Galleria Nazionale).*

After indulging in a five-course meal, many of these foodies head over to GELATERIA LA PILOTTA for the best gelato in the area. Here they mix with locals who have spent their day hanging out across the street on the vast Piazza del Pace. The shop has a funky circular layout and is decorated with multicolored tiles that produce a disco-like ambiance. LA PILOTTA makes a great **bacio di dama**, a chocolate, hazelnut, and cherry swirl literally translated as "lady's kiss," and a refreshing **passion fruit granita**. Besides these delicacies the shop is also **notable for its cone construction.** The process begins with a server packing the cone with your first choice followed by the application of the next flavor in a spackle-like manner around the rim so that the cone grows outward rather than upward. Each subsequent flavor is adeptly applied in this manner so that by the end the finished product is almost as wide as it is tall and incredibly does not fall on one's shoes.

RAVENNA

Ravenna's role as the western seat of Byzantine power has
left a legacy of art and architecture unique in all of Western
Europe. The town is a destination for travelers interested
in viewing the remarkable colored mosaics that can be
found in the churches and tombs of the Byzantine period.

Sorbetteria degli Esarchi

ADDRESS Via IV Novembre 11
PHONE 0544 36315
HOURS 11a–9p daily, closed mid-afternoon
DIRECTIONS *From the central Piazza del Popolo walk north on Via IV Novembre.
The shop is a half block up on the west side of the street.*

SORBETTERIA DEGLI ESARCHI is named in honor
of the *exarches,* the Byzantine viceroys who
ruled the city from the sixth to the eighth
centuries and were responsible for the
proliferation of the mosaics. The shop pays
homage to these rulers with a beautiful
mosaic apse, depicting the meeting of two
birds surrounded by a floral pattern. This
decoration along with its wooden beams, faux
oven, and custom-built counter make it one of
the prettiest gelaterias in Italy. It is hard to believe
that the shop was founded in 1997, for no detail has been
forgotten, from the cones positioned to resemble a flower
arrangement to the perfect stacking of cups along the wall.
SORBETTERIA DEGLI ESARCHI gives hope to all would-be gelato
artisans who are seeking to open a memorable new shop of
their own. The **stracciatella** and **fragola** are my favorites
from their very good selection of flavors.

GELATO LORE

Out of the Dark and into the Cold

While the fall of the Roman Empire marks the beginning of the dark ages for Italian flavored ices, the tradition did continue in other parts of the world and was especially vibrant in China. There is evidence that by the arrival of Marco Polo in the late thirteenth century, the Chinese had been using ice and snow for over 2,500 years for a variety of purposes including the preservation of food, the cooling of houses, and the chilling of drinks. Upon his return to Venice after his epic seventeen-year voyage, Marco Polo is credited with introducing recipes for Chinese flavored ices to Europe. While it is probable that he was exposed to such recipes, there is no documentation to support this claim and in recent years it has been widely refuted by historians who argue that this story was invented in the nineteenth century in an attempt to enrich gelato's historical lineage.

Instead, the reintroduction of flavored ices to Italy is now believed to have occurred during the ninth-century conquest of Sicily by the Moors. Along with agrarian reform and ceramic art, the Moors brought over methods for freezing and flavoring ices. Native Sicilians quickly learned these methods and, utilizing Arabian and indigenous ingredients such as jasmine, almonds, saffron, and lemons, were able to create iced mixtures similar to today's sorbets. As the Italian peninsula once again became prosperous during the fifteenth century, these early gelato artisans began a northern migration, eventually spreading their freezing techniques and secret recipes across the varied regions of Italy.

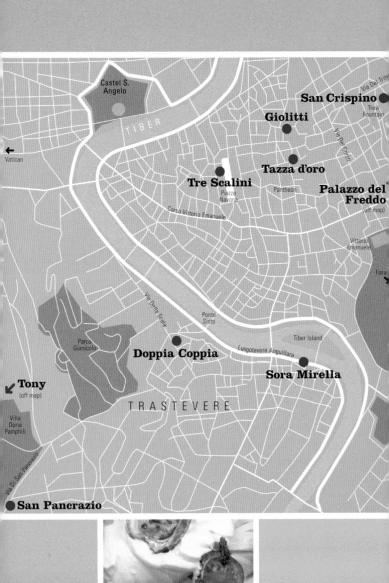

Castel S.
Angelo

San Crispino

Trevi
Fountain

Via Del Tritti

Giolitti

TIBER

Via Del Corso

← Vatican

Tazza d'oro

Tre Scalini

Pantheon

Palazzo del
Freddo

Piazza
Navona

(off map)

Corso Vittorio Emanuele

Vittorio
Emanuele

Via Della Scala

Foru

Ponte
Sisto

Tiber Island

Doppia Coppia

Lungotevere Anguillara

Parco
Gianicolo

Sora Mirella

↙ Tony
(off map)

TRASTEVERE

Villa
Doria
Pamphili

Via D. San Pancrazio

● San Pancrazio

ROME

is a gelato-lovers paradise, where every church, fountain, and ancient site is seemingly flanked by at least one and on occasion several gelaterias. Restaurants, cafés, and street vendors also serve gelato, leaving a visitor with an overabundance of options. To solve this quandary I have listed nine locations, each with its own unique characteristics and delicious specialties. These shops are located throughout Rome, with at least one located a short walk from most of the city's major destinations. A visitor could spend an entire week just touring the sites surrounding these gelaterias, augmenting their reservoir of cultural images as well as the size of their tummies. Do not let this dissuade you from eating as much gelato as you like; you are in Rome, a city that counts a certain amount of decadence a good thing.

Doppia Coppia

ADDRESS Via della Scala 50

PHONE No phone

HOURS Mon–Fri 1p–12a, Sat and Sun 1p–1a, closed December and January

DIRECTIONS *From Piazza Trilussa on the Trastevere side of the Ponte Sisto, walk west on Via Ponte Sisto (which after a block becomes Via S. Dorotea) and take a left onto Via della Scala. The shop is on the next corner at the intersection of Vicola di Bologna.*

Situated on a corner a little ways from the hustle and bustle of the Trastevere night scene, DOPPIA COPPIA (also known as ALLA SCALA) appears at first glance to be no different from the hundreds of other good, but not great, gelaterias in Italy. Do not let the shop's hole-in-the-wall façade fool you; DOPPIA COPPIA makes some of the best gelato in Rome. Due to these cramped quarters, they focus solely on gelato, eschewing secondary gelateria fare such as pastries, cakes, and coffee. This focus results in a refined selection of flavors, of which I believe the **cannella** (cinnamon) to be the best. The true beauty of the shop is realized when, with nowhere to stand or sit after receiving a cone, one must partake in the time-honored tradition of strolling through the magical Trastevere streets. Also in Trastevere is the infamous BAR SAN CALISTO *(Piazza di San Calisto 4)*. This local dive is home to some of Rome's most seedy characters as well as what many claim to be the city's best **cioccolato** gelato.

Gelateria Giolitti

ADDRESS Via degli Uffici del Vicario 40
PHONE 06 6991243
HOURS 7a–2a daily
DIRECTIONS *From the Piazza della Rotonda (Pantheon) walk north on Via del Pantheon until it turns into Via della Maddalena. Follow Via della Maddalena until it ends and take a right onto Via degli Uffici del Vicario. The shop's bright sign is immediately visible.*

No one can truly talk gelato until they have sampled GIOLITTI's offerings. A yardstick for all other Roman gelaterias, even its detractors feel the need to describe their favorite gelateria as "better than GIOLITTI." While some say the gelato is no longer the best in town, nearly everyone admits that the locale provides the best gelato experience. After waiting in line to pay the cashier and fighting through Italian families and Japanese tour groups to get to the counter, one is presented with a choice of over fifty fresh flavors. Perhaps more important than these selections is the large bowl mounted on the back counter. Inside its beautiful shell rests the tastiest **panna montata** (whipped cream) known to man. All one needs to say to get a healthy dollop on top of your cone is a soft spoken *"con panna"* (with cream) at the end of an order, but I have heard this shrieked in succession by a spectrum of people ranging from little girls to burly men, all afraid that their cone will not be topped off with this nectar of the gods. The shop's flavors are all superb and, as you are in the best of hands, I suggest you explore on your own what makes this a gelateria of legend.

Gelateria San Crispino

ADDRESS   Via della Panetteria 42
PHONE   06 6793924
HOURS   Sun, Mon, Wed–Thu 12p–12:30a, Fri–Sat 12p–1:30a, closed Tue
DIRECTIONS   *From the Trevi Fountain walk east two blocks on Via del Lavatore and take a left onto Via della Panetteria.*

This Zen-like gelateria is welcome not only for providing an oasis of calm from the nearby chaos of the Trevi Fountain but also for its singular attention to the task at hand, making delicious gelato. A California-meets-Rome aura abounds here, with classical music, pastel walls, and a detailed menu combining to create an atmosphere akin to a nouveau restaurant. After being soothed by the ambience, one must choose from an array of what many, including the *New York Times, Gourmet* magazine, and several Italian periodicals, claim to be the best flavors in Rome. The shop's secret to success is its ever-changing menu that is updated throughout the year to make room for various seasonal delicacies. Great pride goes into production of each flavor and only the finest and freshest ingredients, from saffron to licorice, are chosen. The shop is so dedicated to pleasing your palate that it **only serves its gelato in cups,** claiming that cones interfere with the subtlety of their flavors. Depending on the time of year I recommend the **mirtillo** (blueberry) and the **ricotta**. If these flavors are not on the menu do not despair because the shop's **Il Gelato di San Crispino** — a crema and honey blend — is available year round and I guarantee it will be among the tastiest gelato you have ever tried.

I Tre Scalini

ADDRESS Piazza Navona, 28-32
PHONE 06 68801996
HOURS 8a–1a, closed Wed, January
DIRECTIONS *On the west side of the Piazza, just north of the Fontana dei Quattro Fiumi.*

In the center of Piazza Navona, TRE SCALINI is a full-service restaurant with over 50 outdoor tables that can accommodate hordes of tourists. Although the food is good (though pricey) the restaurant distinguishes itself from others on the square by adhering to the time-honored saying — "location, location, *tartufo.*" TRE SCALINI'S **tartufo** consists of chunks of rich chocolate and candied sour cherries encased in a ball of chocolate gelato and topped with a mound of whipped cream and chocolate bits. It is widely considered the best tartufo in Rome and has made the restaurant a magnet for chocolate lovers throughout the world. Try to sit at the outer ring of tables, which provide the best view of Bernini's Quattro Fiumi fountain as well as some of the best people watching in the city. Be aware of the copycat restaurant next door that offers an inferior product. If chocolate is not your thing, then the nearby DA QUINTO GELATERIA *(Via di Tor Millina 15)* makes a delicious **frullato**, the Italian version of the smoothie.

Palazzo del Freddo di Giovanni Fassi

ADDRESS Via Principe Eugenio 65/67
PHONE 06 4464740
HOURS Sun 10a–12a, Tue–Fri 12p–12a, Sat 12p–1a, closed Mon
DIRECTIONS *South of the train station, two blocks away from the northeastern corner of Piazza Vittorio Emanuele, between Via Cairoli and Via Nino Bixio.*

PALAZZO DEL FREDDO DI GIOVANNI FASSI shines like a beacon of light from the surrounding apartments and shops of Rome's immigrant community. The beautifully maintained building has been the home of this shop for the past seventy-five years, while the business itself was begun back in 1880. It truly feels like you have walked into a gelato palace after entering and viewing the vast hall set aside for customers to order, sit, and eat. The shop never forgets that eating gelato is a treat and thus uses this large space to create a quirky atmosphere, reminiscent of Willy Wonka's chocolate factory. Plastic fruit hangs from the ceiling, old gelato carts and makers are on display, and Latin inscriptions are cut into the walls. The gelato is so good that the shop also functions as a factory, shipping its products to markets and restaurants throughout the region. Of their many choices I recommend the sinful **nutella**, made with Italy's favorite hazelnut spread, and the potent **noce** (walnut). While the shop is not on the path of the traditional tourist routes, its proximity to the train station makes it a perfect diversion for those who find themselves waiting for a connection for an hour or more, a common enough occurrence for anyone traveling through Italy.

San Pancrazio

ADDRESS   Piazza San Pancrazio 17–18
PHONE   06 58310338
HOURS   Fluctuate
DIRECTIONS   *On the Janiculum across from the entrance to the Doria Pamphili park, just south of the intersection of Via di San Pancrazio and Via Fonteiana.*

When Romans want to escape the heat and congestion of the city streets they flee up the Janiculum to the sprawling Villa Doria Pamphili. SAN PANCRAZIO is strategically placed near the entrance of the park's southeastern gate, affording visitors the opportunity to stroll with a cone or stop for a treat after a jog. It's worth the trip throughout the year, but is best visited on *Pasquetta* (Easter Monday). On this day locals, following the tradition of picnicking outside the city walls, transform the park from a quiet place perfect for long walks into a mass gathering of Romans sipping white wine, finishing off Easter leftovers, and playing soccer. For dessert it seems as though the whole of Rome visits SAN PANCRAZIO for a taste of its gelato. I enjoyed the **mandorla e pinola** (almond and pine nut) and the **pistacchio**, but the reason for the post-Easter feeding frenzy is the house specialty, **Ciambellone San Pancrazio**. This heavenly flavor tastes like a cross between lemon meringue pie and a sugar donut and is reason enough to venture outside the walls.

Sora Mirella la Grattachecca

ADDRESS On the Lungotevere degli Anguillara

PHONE No phone

HOURS 9a–1a and beyond, hours vary according to weather, open only during high season

DIRECTIONS *On the Trastevere side of the Ponte Cestio, just across from Tiber Island.*

Since 1915, Sora Mirella la Grattachecca has proudly carried on the Italian shaved-ice tradition from its prime position overlooking Tiber Island. Always a favorite of locals and tourists seeking an escape from the hot Roman sun along this shady bank of the river, the shop has become even more popular with the inauguration of a ferry service in the spring of 2003. During the weekends, the lines in front of the shop mirror the lines for the boat and grow even larger during the wee hours long after the boat service has stopped running. Line is probably the wrong word however, because the groups of people gathered in front more often resemble a rugby scrum. Do not let this deter you, despite the maneuvers of older women and young children, both masters of getting to the front of Italian lines, you will get your chance to order in due time. The servers maintain a Tao-like serenity amidst this chaos, calmly waiting until the person shaving the ice has filled a cup before they add the delicious flavorings. Somehow watching this methodical process makes the wait enjoyable and also lets you get a peak at some of the flavors. I enjoy the **lampone** (raspberry), **mirtillo**, and the **fragola** — which has the added bonus of being topped by sugared, semi-frozen strawberries.

Tazza d'Oro

ADDRESS   Via degli Orfani 84
PHONE   06 6789792
HOURS   7a–8p, closed Sun
DIRECTIONS   *On the east side of Piazza della Rotonda, a stone's throw from the Pantheon.*

Two things Romans love to do are talk and drink coffee, so if the topic about the best coffee in Rome rises, get ready for a long, passionate discussion. After all is said and done, more than likely there will be two cafés left standing: CAFÉ SANT'EUSTACHIO and TAZZA D'ORO. The former wins points for its *Gran Caffè*, which utilizes a secret formula that produces a sugary flavor and an incredibly creamy head of foam, while the latter is famous for its house blend of imported beans and frothy, strong *cappuccino*. The question of which is better is a topic for another book, but I can say that TAZZA D'ORO is my favorite because of its other specialty, **granita di caffè**. The beauty of this delight is its simplicity, comprised solely of frozen, slightly sugared coffee encased in two dollops of unsweetened whipped cream. While the temptation to get the granita to-go in order to explore the Pantheon may be strong, I suggest eating it right at the bar out of a long glass among the Italians that make this their second home. The Pantheon will still be there after you are done and the granita pick-me-up guarantees a boost of energy. Make sure to pay at the cashier first and then walk to the opposite end of the bar (towards the Pantheon), the only section that serves the granita.

Tony

ADDRESS Largo Missiroli Alberto 17
PHONE 06 58201002
HOURS Fluctuate, closed Mon
DIRECTIONS *In Monteverde west of S. Camillo hospital off of Via dei Colli Portuensi.*

Do not try to find TONY, **TONY must find you.** In the heart of Monteverde away from the city's major sites and attractions is Rome's current gelateria of choice. Unfortunately, even the savviest of travelers must rely on a good cabbie or Italian friend to find the shop. If you are lucky enough to be taken there, you might glance at the servers behind the counter and do a double take, thinking you have entered a butcher shop by mistake. It is one thing to have a man or a couple of teenagers behind the counter, but when a gelateria can support a group of four to five men-type-men, then the gelato will always be memorable. Such is the case at TONY, with gelato so beloved that even the gracious Romans have tried to keep it a secret. The shop's specialty is the **"spaghetti,"** a carton filled with a bed of fresh whipped cream and topped with gelato that is pressed through a strainer to resemble a clump of noodles. It is tough to recommend one flavor over another here as they are all delicious, but if pushed I would suggest the **crema**, **nutella**, and **spagnola** — similar to the more common amerena, a cherry swirl concoction.

Bigo

La Cremeria
della Erbe

Palazzo
Ducale

Piazza de
Ferrari

Piazza
Dante

Giorgelato

Via XX Settembre

Via Colombo

Via Cesarea

Balilla

Via Macaggi

GULF OF
GENOA

GENOA's recent urban renewal

program has transformed its once seedy harbor
into a quasi-amusement park, complete with
shops, movie theaters, restaurants, rides, ice
skating, an aquarium and, most important,
several gelaterias. While none of these waterfront
gelaterias are noteworthy, their multitude is a
testament to the city's proud gelato heritage.
To find the exemplars of this heritage you must
venture into Genoa's cavernous streets. The three
shops listed here hark back to the glory days of
the city's naval supremacy, where grandiose tastes
left an architectural heritage of magnificent
palaces jutting into the sky. Any of these gelaterias
would have pleased the palates of bygone naval
heroes and wealthy merchants as they do
contemporary Genovese citizens.

Balilla 🪑 ☀ 🐎

ADDRESS Via Macaggi 84

PHONE 010 542161

HOURS Sun 7:30a–9p, Tue–Sat 7:30a–12a, closed Mon

DIRECTIONS *From Piazza de Ferrari walk east on Via XX Settembre and take a right onto Via Cesarea. The shop is located in the southeastern part of town at the intersection of Via Macaggi and Via Cesarea.*

A pleasant walk from the old city center, BALILLA is the first place I like to visit on arriving in Genoa. The shop is named for the eighteenth-century Genovese boy who is said to have thrown a pebble at an Austrian official, thus sparking a revolt that led to the withdrawal of the occupying Austrians. This story continues to be a source of pride for the modern-day Genovese, as does this remarkable gelateria.

BALILLA is a throwback to early twentieth-century elegance, reminiscent of American malt shops and drugstores of a bygone era. With leather-backed chairs, dainty pink tablecloths, marble floors, and wood counters, BALILLA would be worth the trip even if its offerings were average. But that is not the case — its gelato is devastating. It seems like the white-jacketed servers are performing magic as they guide the flavors from canisters to cones while the gelato hangs off the spoons a good six inches without a drop. This notable consistency is the mark of a premier gelateria. All the flavors here are great but I especially enjoyed the **panera**, a coffee and crema blend unique to Liguria, and the **crema catalana**, like crème brûlée in a cone.

Giorgelato

ADDRESS	Via Colombo 177
PHONE	No phone
HOURS	Fluctuate
DIRECTIONS	*From Piazza de Ferrari walk east on Via XX Settembre and take a left onto Via Colombo. The shop is on the west side of the street.*

During evening hours on this busy pedestrian street a carnival atmosphere pervades, with Genovese going about their daily errands in the midst of street performers and wandering tourists. Packed in amongst the jugglers, dog circus, clothing stores, and specialty food merchants is GIORGELATO's tiny storefront. The shop's devoted clientele count a visit to GIORGELATO, which has been serving customers since 1926, as part of their daily ritual, as common as buying groceries or window shopping. While its small selection of flavors are very good, the real reason for its continued prosperity lies with the owners and employees. Of all the places I visited, GIORGELATO had the friendliest servers, willingly making suggestions, giving samples, and listing ingredients of any unusual flavors. Everyone should be so lucky to have this little shop as a local gelateria. Try the **giandiua**, a chocolate and hazelnut blend that tastes like Rocky Road without the marshmallows, or the unbeatable **fior di latte** (pure rich milk and sugar).

La Cremeria delle Erbe

ADDRESS Vico delle Erbe 15
PHONE 010 2469254
HOURS Mon 11a–9p, Tue–Thu 11a–1a, Fri–Sun 11a–2a
DIRECTIONS *From the Piazza Matteotti (in front of the Palazzo Ducale) walk south on Vico delle Erbe. The shop is located on the west side of the Piazza delle Erbe.*

LA CREMERIA DELLE ERBE is situated in a lively square just a short walk from the Palazzo Ducale. Full of outdoor restaurants and bars, the piazza is a popular nightspot for Genovese and travelers alike. In keeping with the surrounding ambiance, the shop serves granita-based mixed drinks as well as gelato. The Russian-inspired **granitoski** and South American-influenced **capiritissima** are fruity granitas mixed respectively with vodka and rum. Tasty and refreshing, the drinks have the overall effect of a loaded slushy. For those interested in an alcohol-free treat, I suggest the **cioccolato al pepe**, chocolate with a hint of pepper that, while subtle at first, leaves a pleasing peppery flavor in your mouth long after the cone is finished. Berry lovers will enjoy the **frutti di bosco** (mixed berries) which is so condensed that it seems to be more jam than gelato.

TIPS & INFO

Go-to cone

Even the most urbane of travelers has a difficult time blending into today's ultrahip Italian scene. As a rather tall, pale American living in Italy, it took me a while to shake the feeling that everyone was staring at me. After a while I learned a few techniques that made assimilation, if not seamless, at least less awkward. I pass these techniques on with the hope that you will not have to endure flashbacks to a gawky seventh-grade past while walking the Italian streets.

THE FIRST thing I do upon arriving in Italy is to observe what type of **sunglasses** the trendiest of Italians are wearing so I can purchase similar knock-offs from a street vendor. My general rule of thumb is to pick out a pair that make me feel slightly uncomfortable and that I would be openly mocked for wearing back home.

NEXT, I unpack my trusty **motorino (scooter) helmet** and begin carrying it with me at all times. The helmets can be bought for about twenty dollars and are a necessary accessory regardless of whether you have a motorino or not. I noticed the first time I carried one around that my credibility was instantly bolstered and, depending on my level of tan/swarthiness, had people confusing me for a local or at worst an expatriate.

FINALLY, when visiting a gelateria, I always make sure that I can rattle off a predetermined assortment of commonly available flavors, or as I like to call it, a **go-to cone.** It is a hot summer night, the crowd is ten deep and suddenly you find yourself face to face with a *gelataio* (server or gelato artisan) who looks as though he may come after you with his spoon if you don't tell him what you want right then and there. Most travelers wilt under this pressure, missing their chance to order, relegated to the back of the line, and blowing any illusions that they are frequent customers. The go-to cone alleviates this problem by providing an easily remembered order for any occasion.

Having a go-to cone is not an excuse to order the same thing again and again and thus spoil the time-honored tradition of trying out new and unique flavors; rather, it is a way to fool onlookers into thinking that you know what you are doing in times of pressure.

Fiera di
Milano

Parco
Sempione

Arena

Viel

Giardini
Pubblici

Castello
Sforzesco

Pinacoteca
di Brera

Corso Giuseppe Garibaldi

Via Monastro

**Gelateria
Toldo**

Piazza de
Angeli

Via Marghera

**Gelateria
Marghera**

Duomo

Università

Corso di Porta Ticinese

Viale Cortina

Piazza XXIV Maggio

Ripa di Porta Ticinese

**Gelateria
Rinomata**

MILAN's dual role as Italy's fashion

capital and international business hub has created a city with an unparalleled metropolitan sophistication. Maintaining a mix of Northern European industriousness and high Italian culture, the city's residents work hard and look good doing it. This style has created a unique gelato culture, in which appearance and substance vie for top billing.

During the day appearance is at a premium, when workers meet at trendy cafés and gourmet food stores to sip coffee and eat gelato. At night, however, inhibitions are relaxed and people stroll from one cool restaurant or bar to the next, stopping at gelaterias in between. While you may feel uncomfortable in a city where most people own pairs of jeans that are more expensive than your entire wardrobe, fear not, as even the coolest of customers transforms into a kid while surveying choices and placing an order. Visit these shops, relax, and enjoy the opportunity to interact with the Milanese at their best.

Gelateria Marghera

ADDRESS Via Marghera 33
PHONE 02 48194332
HOURS 10a–1a daily
DIRECTIONS *In the western part of the city center between the Wagner and De Angeli metro stops.*

Call it a bias, but in general I do not like to recommend any of what I call the "bright" gelato shops, with incandescent lighting and huge tubs of gelato displayed in modern steel-and-glass refrigeration units. These new shops not only lack the character and beauty of the classic gelaterias, but also generally serve an inferior product. GELATERIA MARGHERA, however, is the exception to this rule. Instead of the sterile feeling so prevalent in bright shops, MARGHERA generates a lively atmosphere while producing memorable gelato. The tub of the tasty **amarena**, fior di latte mixed with cherry, is so large you feel like going for a swim, and the refreshing **mandarino cinese** (Chinese mandarin), complete with bits of rind, is one of many unusual flavors that add to this shop's appeal. For purists who can't bear to visit the bright locales, the nearby CREMERIA BUONARROTI *(Via Buonarroti 9)* is an old-school gelateria with outdoor seating at the entrance to the Wagner metro stop.

Gelateria Rinomata

ADDRESS Ripa di Porta Ticinese 2

PHONE 02 58113877

HOURS 1p–1a, closed Mon afternoon from October–May

DIRECTIONS *In the Naviglio district in the southern part of the city center just west of the Piazza XXIV Maggio. From the Porta Genova metro stop walk east on Via Vigevano until it merges with Viale Gorizia. The shop is on the corner of Gorizia and Ripa di Porta Ticinese.*

GELATERIA RINOMATA is at the literal and figurative crossroads of southern Milan. At an intersection of several roads and the city's canal network, the area is a mix of blue-collar neighborhoods and a multitude of restaurants and bars that set up shop and breathed new life into the area. The effect of all of these junctions is a lively buzz, a St. Petersburg-meets Greenwich Village aura. Twenty- and thirty-something Milanese use the gelateria as a meeting spot, congregating in front and adding to the shop's vibe. Once inside you can see that everything is done with care, from the floor-to-ceiling glass-and-wood cabinets holding hundreds of stacked cones to the fancy brass coverlets preserving the gelato. This appearance does not disappoint, as the gelato lives up to its surroundings. Highlights include the **mela verda** (green apple) and the **fragola con nutella** (strawberry with nutella).

Gelateria Toldo

ADDRESS Via Ponte Vetero 11

PHONE 02 86460863

HOURS 7a–9p, closed Sun and Aug 14–24

DIRECTIONS *In the Brera district, a five- to ten-minute walk from either the Cairoli or Cordusio metro stops. From Cairoli walk east on Via Cusani and take your first left onto Via Ponte Vetero. From Cordusio walk north on Via Broletto until it eventually becomes Via Ponte Vetero.*

GELATERIA TOLDO is one of those unique places that function as a window into the soul of the city in which it is located. Set on a charming street across the way from a fancy *pescheria* (a seafood merchant whose fresh selections are definitely worth a peak), TOLDO is elegant while still maintaining the hipness that personifies modern-day Milan. This mixture of style and cool pervades throughout, from the elongated mod light fixtures to the well-dressed clientele that frequent the shop for cappuccinos in the morning and gelato from noon till close. TOLDO'S selection is delicious with standouts including the **stracciatella**, the unusual **soia, sesamo e pinolo** (soy, sesame, and pine nut) and the **Jamaica**, a rich chocolate mixed with rum and bits of sponge cake.

Viel

ADDRESS Corso Garibaldi 12
PHONE 02 86915489
HOURS Sun–Tue, Thu, Fri 8a–1a, Sat 8a–2a, closed Wed
DIRECTIONS *Near the Arena, south of the Moscova metro stop between Via Palermo and Piazza San Simpliciano.*

With multiple locations spread throughout the city, a ubiquitous palm tree logo, and fruit, such as pineapples and bananas, displayed for all to see, VIEL is trying its best to bring a little bit of the tropics to downtown Milan. Opened in 1948, the business has always placed a premium on fresh, natural ingredients, adhering to the motto, *la qualità della natura* (the quality of nature). The *Garibaldi* shop is the best located of the bunch and caters to pedestrians looking for a treat after a walk in the nearby Parco Sempione. Though VIEL's gelato is good, I recommend one of their **macedonie**, inspired fruit cocktails, or a **frullato**, a cross between a milk shake and a smoothie. The shop's specialty is the **frullato misto**, a secret blend of fresh fruits and gelato that is as refreshing as a tropical breeze.

Fiorio

Pepino

Caffè Miretti

Giardino
Reale

Piazza
Castello

Teatro
Regio

Via Principe Amedeo

Palazzo
Carignano

Via Po

Via Bogino

Piazza
Carlo
Emanuele

Corso Re Umberto

Corso Matteotti

Via Arsenale

Piazza
Carlo
Felice

Stazione
Porta
Nuova

Corso Vittorio Emanuele II

TURIN

With their orderly grid and uniform architecture, the streets of Turin embody the industrious spirit of its denizens. Home to car manufacturer Fiat and perennial soccer champion Juventus as well as a famous Egyptian museum and the shroud of Turin, the city takes pride in both its blue-collar work ethic and impressive cultural heritage. This pride is evident in the current effort by residents to restore the city's fading luster in time for the 2006 Winter Olympics. As you would expect, the city also celebrates its strong gelato tradition. It is very difficult to have even average gelato in Turin, as the continued success of several grand old cafés and century-old gelaterias have set a citywide gelato standard unparalleled in all of Italy.

Caffè Miretti 🐦

ADDRESS Corso Matteotti 5

PHONE 011 533687

HOURS Sun 8a–2a, Tue–Fri 7a–1:30a, Sat and holidays 7a–2a, closed Mon

DIRECTIONS *In the southwestern part of the city center, between Via dell' Arsenale and Via Venti Settembre.*

Situated on a nondescript street west of the Piazza San Carlo and other main attractions, CAFFÈ MIRETTI may be one of the best-kept secrets in town. On first impression the shop appears to be another elegant Italian café that focuses on espressos and cappuccinos and serves gelato as an afterthought. This however is not the case, as MIRETTI produces some of the best gelato I have ever had. One hint that the shop makes good gelato is the abundance of customers arriving via *motorini* (scooters). There are gelaterias within walking distance from almost any point of the city, so the presence of scooters means that rather than visit a neighborhood shop people would sooner strap on a helmet and drive to MIRETTI. After tasting its flavors I cannot say that I blame them. The gelato is of the type that does not lend itself to being scooped, rather it is swirled onto the cone as it slowly falls off the spoon. The **zabaione con amaretti**, a custard-like vanilla with a hint of amaretto, and the **crema arancia**, a creamy orange flavor with bits of jellied rind and a hint of Grand Marnier, are reason enough to visit MIRETTI, be it from the other side of town or across the Atlantic.

Fiorio

ADDRESS	Via Po 8
PHONE	011 8170612
HOURS	8a–12a, closed Mon
DIRECTIONS	*From the Piazza Castello walk east on Via Po. The shop is on the corner of Via Po and Via Bogino.*

When walking under the covered portico on the Via Po during summer evenings it seems as though every other person is walking with a cone in hand. This is not a coincidence, but a result of people going out of their way to make sure they pass FIORIO during their evening *passeggiata* (stroll). When the temperature begins to drop, customers stop ordering from the window on Via Bogino and retreat inside to order from the elegant marble bar or be served in the aperitivo room. This cozy, red velvet room is adorned with a painted ceiling, intricate molding, and a chandelier. Because of its relatively small selection (~14 choices) and immense popularity, the shop is able to replenish its flavors frequently, ensuring a freshness that is not found at many other gelaterias. My favorites include the **cocco** (coconut), similar to a condensed piña colada, and the **pesca** (peach), tasting as fresh as if it were made a minute prior to ordering.

Pepino

ADDRESS	Piazza Carignano 8
PHONE	011 542009
HOURS	8a–12a daily
DIRECTIONS	*In the center of town, abutting the Teatro Carignano and facing the Palazzo Carignano (the Risorgimento Museum).*

During the end of the nineteenth century, the Piazza Carignano was a meeting point for leaders of the *Risorgimento* — Italy's reunification movement. Over the last hundred years people have continued the tradition of assembling in this square, not, however, to discuss politics, but to visit PEPINO, the granddaddy of Turin's proud gelato tradition. Open since 1884, the shop's fame has grown to the point where today you can find PEPINO-branded products sold at nonaffiliated cafés and markets throughout the city. Of all the shop's scrumptious offerings, including a tangy **albicocca** (apricot), the **penguino** remains the most popular. This cherished creation consists of pure vanilla gelato placed on a stick and dipped in rich milk chocolate. Order one of these delicacies and you may be inspired to start your own movement, back to the counter for a second helping.

GELATO LORE

The Chicken and the Queen

The story behind the introduction of sorbets to France remains one of the most interesting gelato tales. In early sixteenth-century Florence, a man, known only today as Ruggeri, won a cooking competition with a flavored ice sculpture submission.

As a chicken farmer who dabbled in long-forgotten recipes, Ruggeri was unprepared for the sudden fame that the award brought him. Caterina de' Medici the fourteen-year-old fiancé of Henry of Orleans (the future king of France), requested that Ruggeri join her bridal entourage along with her ladies-in-waiting, artists, perfumists, and other consorts. Having no choice, Ruggeri accompanied the future queen to Marseilles, where he prepared a sorbet-like ice sculpture for her wedding banquet.

The sculpture caused such a stir that soon his creations were displayed at all of Caterina's banquets and were the talk of the royal court. Anxious to replicate these wonders, other royal chefs began to pester Ruggeri for the secrets to his technique, but Ruggeri refused to divulge any information. Soon the other chefs became so angry and jealous that they attacked and beat him.

Fearing for his life and homesick for Florence, Ruggeri pleaded with Caterina and eventually struck a deal: he would turn over his secret recipes in exchange for being allowed to return to Italy and live out his life in the company of his chickens.

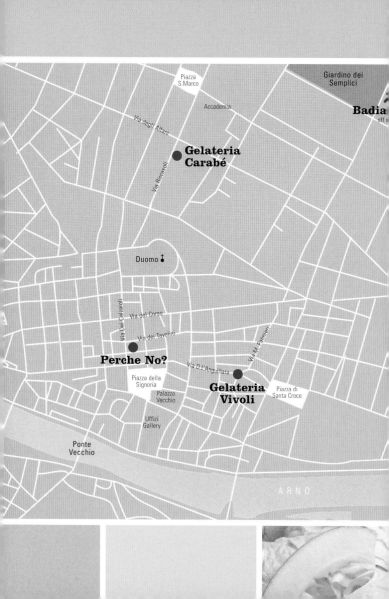

FLORENCE, the cradle of the Italian

Renaissance, has for centuries drawn travelers
yearning to view its artistic treasure. The city's vast
booty has consequently created a thriving tourist
industry that caters to millions of visitors from
around the globe each year. While the crowds
may be overwhelming at times, a benefit of the
city's popularity is the abundance
of charming restaurants, high-
fashion stores and bargain-priced
merchants open to serve the
constant tide of tourists.

Likewise, Florence is blessed
with several great gelaterias,
each with its own distinct tradition and feel. The only problem
for gelato connoisseurs is that in
order to find the worthwhile
shops one must ignore the siren
songs of the multitude of mediocre gelaterias that
seems to be on every corner. Be strong: I assure you
that the following shops are the best in town, and the
city is small enough for you to walk to at least one
of them from any location within minutes. There is
therefore no reason to fall prey to an average cone.

Badiani 🐴

ADDRESS Viale dei Mille 20/r
PHONE 055 578682
HOURS 7a–1a, closed Tue
DIRECTIONS *Northeast of the city center in the vicinity of the Stadio Comunale and Campo di Marte train station, on the corner of Viale dei Mille and Via Nino Bixio.*

Usually I do not like to recommend shops that are not located within city centers or near notable attractions, but sometimes a place is just too good to omit. For over seventy years, BADIANI has been a local favorite, but it was not until 1970 that it became a destination for all Florentines. In that year the city held a competition in honor of Bernardo Buontalenti, the famous architect of the Medici court who, among other projects, had a hand in the design of the Uffizi Gallery. As contestants throughout the city prepared submissions for the contest, BADIANI decided to pay homage to Buontalenti's other contribution to society — his vital role in the evolution of gelato (for more information see page 67). BADIANI's submission won first prize and from that moment on their **Buontalenti** flavor — a secret recipe that is similar to, but better than, **fior di panna** (rich cream and sugar) — has attracted crowds and pleased palates. Another Florentine favorite is the nearby CAVINI *(Piazza delle Cure)*, which despite its facing one of the uglier piazzas in Florence, has a small but vocal constituency that considers its gelato the best in town.

Gelateria Carabé ₿

ADDRESS Via Ricasoli 60/r
PHONE 055 289476
HOURS Feb 15–May 15, Oct 1–Nov 15: Tue–Sun 10a–8p,
May 16–Sep 30: 10a–12a daily
DIRECTIONS *Halfway between the Accademia and the Duomo on the east side
of the street. Also a Forte dei Marmi location at Via P.I. da Carrara 23/d.*

Antonio Lisciandro, a self-described "walking encyclopedia of gelato," brings three generations of gelato knowledge and secrets from his native Sicily to the heart of Florence. Together with his wife Loredana, the couple has created a third must-visit destination on this street that connects the Piazza del Duomo with the Accademia. While Brunelleschi's dome and Michelangelo's David inspire awe at first sight, CARABÉ's goods must first be tasted to be truly appreciated. A drab exterior leads to a selection of muted gelato and granita that is stored in stainless steel containers rather than one of the swirling machines common to most gelaterias. This lack of pizzazz is not a reason for concern; instead it is a testament to the shop's practice of using only the freshest ingredients. The gelato may not be as bright as others, but that is because no preservatives or artificial flavorings have been added. Similarly, the granita is made fresh daily and thus does not have to be constantly rotated. Antonio imports "bumpy" lemons — the large version of the fruit that is Sicily's culinary calling card — every week during high season and uses them to produce the best **limone granita** I have ever had — a perfect combination of lemon, ice, and sugar that dissolves in your mouth on first taste. Another Sicilian specialty on hand is the **pistacchio** gelato, a creamy marvel that far surpasses other shops' versions.

Gelateria Vivoli 🏦 ☀

ADDRESS Via Isola delle Stinche 7/r

PHONE 055 292334

HOURS Sun 9:30a–12a, Mon and Wed–Sat 7:30a–12a,
closed Tue, most of January and August

DIRECTIONS *From the northeast corner of Piazza S. Firenze (just east of Piazza
della Signoria), walk east on Via della Vigna Vecchia until it intersects
Via Isola delle Stinche. From Piazza di Santa Croce walk west on
Via Torta and take the first right onto Via Isola delle Stinche.
The shop is on the west side of the street.*

The New York Yankees of gelato, this small shop is
perhaps the most famous gelateria in all of Italy. Much
like the Yankees, VIVOLI has both crazed, loyal followers
proclaiming it to be the world's best and detractors who
claim that its quality has not been high for years and it
is merely living off past glory. Whichever camp one falls
into it is hard to ignore the constant stream of customers
who navigate through the pleasant back streets to
frequent the shop at all hours of the day. In my opinion
the gelato is still among the best, but I suggest that
you make the prerequisite pilgrimage to determine
for yourself whether the hype is justified. The shop's
specialties include an amazing **riso** (rice) and the
aranciotti al cioccolato, a candied orange peel topped
with chocolate gelato. In addition to these, VIVOLI serves
devastating mousse concoctions, with my favorites being
the **mousse di amaretto** and the **mousse alle fragole**
(strawberry mousse).

GELATO LORE

Gelato's Renaissance Man

From the early fourteenth century to the end of the sixteenth century, Florence was a hotbed of artistic, architectural, and cultural achievement. This atmosphere spawned many a genius, but few with as tasty a contribution as Bernardo Buontalenti (ca. 1531–1608).

The epitome of a Renaissance man, Buontalenti worked as an architect, designer, inventor and, most important, gelato pioneer. His impressive architectural projects for the Medici court, including the famous octagonal Tribuna in the Uffizi Gallery, would have been enough to earn him lasting distinction, but his true brilliance was as a water engineer — designing fountains, harbors, and ice houses (one of which is still standing in the Boboli Gardens). These ice houses were increasingly popular as Florentines became accustomed to using snow and ice for both storage and gastronomy. Buontalenti capitalized on this burgeoning practice by obtaining the sole concession to bring and sell snow within the city limits.

With a lucrative business secured and ice on his brain, Buontalenti returned to his workshop to satiate his inventive curiosity. In a moment of inspirational genius, Buontalenti partially froze a mixture of milk, honey, egg yolk, and wine, thus creating the precursor to modern-day gelato. So important was his contribution that Tuscan gelaterias still pay homage to this native son by serving the **Buontalenti** flavor, a rich cream-and-egg concoction with a hint of Marsala wine.

Perché No?

ADDRESS Via dei Tavolini 19/r
PHONE 055 2398969
HOURS High season open 10a–1a, off season open 10a–8p, closed Tue
DIRECTIONS *From the Duomo walk south on Via dei Calzaioli and take the third left onto Tavolini.*

PERCHÉ NO? (why not?) is situated in the heart of Florence, halfway between the Duomo and the Piazza della Signoria and just off Via Dei Calzaioli, the city's main artery since the middle ages. This ideal location generates nonstop foot traffic and is one of the reasons the shop continues to be a favorite for both Florentines and tourists alike. The shop was founded in 1939, but rather than appear like the historic gelateria that it is, PERCHÉ NO? has been redesigned to attract a trendier clientele. The custom-built gelato counter, amber clock, mosaic floors, and jazz playing in the background help make this place the coolest gelateria in town. You may think that a shop this concerned with its image may not be focusing enough on the task at hand, but worry not, the gelato is exceptional. The "laboratory" in back produces a wide array of flavors both traditional and unique. I especially enjoyed the fresh **lampone**, the **coffee crunch**, coffee with chunks of chocolate, and the sublime **miele e sesamo** (honey and sesame).

LUCCA

Within its perfectly intact ramparts, Lucca remains one of the most beautiful small towns in Italy. The city's near ban on car traffic creates a serene atmosphere with pedestrians and bikers roaming unencumbered through the streets.

Gelateria Veneta

ADDRESS	Via Vittorio Veneto 74
PHONE	0583 467037
HOURS	10a–1a daily
DIRECTIONS	*The shop is in the southwestern part of town. From Piazza Napoleone walk south a few blocks on Via Veneto. Other shops located at Via Beccheria 10 and Chiasso Barletti 23.*

If you walk these streets long enough you will eventually pass one of GELATERIA VENETA's three locations. This mini-chain was founded in 1927 and today is Lucca's reigning king of gelato, complete with branded ice cream bars and freezer bags. The shop dishes out tiny scoops, which seems chintzy until you realize that you are given three choices rather than the traditional two for a small cone. This extra choice comes in handy as the shop has an ample selection of flavors to choose from. I enjoyed the **pinolata** (pine nut), the **pera** (pear), and the **panna gelata** — an ultra-creamy concoction. While all three shops serve the same flavors, I prefer the original Via Veneto location because of its seating area and proximity to the tree-lined Piazza Napoleone.

PISA

Pisa's Piazza del Duomo, aptly called the Campo dei Miracoli (field of miracles) by the Italians, is a sight so spectacular that everything else, including gelato, is secondary. The Duomo, Baptistery, and world-famous Campanile (Leaning Tower) dazzle hordes of visitors throughout the year and are the sole destination for many travelers to this town.

Caffè Duomo

ADDRESS	Via Santa Maria 114
PHONE	050 561918
HOURS	8a–7:30p, closed Thu
DIRECTIONS	*On the southeast corner of the Piazza del Duomo.*

For this reason I have chosen to recommend CAFFÈ DUOMO. This bar/café occupies the best possible location on the square, with views of all three monuments and a constant sea breeze wafting across the outdoor tables. The gelato here is only decent, but well worth it as you sit in the line of the Campanile's slant, pondering whether you would be crushed should the tower fall. I recommend the basics here, including the **cioccolato** and the **crema**. If you are staying in town for a night or more, GELATERIA ORSO BIANCO *(Via Francesco Crispi 51)* was recently voted the best in town.

SAN GIMIGNANO

This perfectly preserved hilltop town with its famous towers jutting skyward is an ideal daytrip for vacationers stationed in Florence, Siena, or the surrounding Tuscan countryside. The town's ironic fate is that the same towers and fortifications that were built during medieval times to keep marauding hordes out are now the very reason that the town is inundated with tourists during high season.

Gelateria di "Piazza" ₿ 🌅

ADDRESS	Piazza della Cisterna 4
PHONE	0577 942244
HOURS	9a–12a daily, closed November–February
DIRECTIONS	*On the west side of one of the town's two central piazzas.*

Within this maze of towers and fanny packs is the GELATERIA DI "PIAZZA," one of the most renowned gelaterias in Italy. The shop has won numerous awards — most recently the 2003 *coppa del mondo della gelato* (gelato world cup) in Turin — and its walls are covered with articles and photographs praising its unique flavors. Among these are the smooth **banana**, the **vernaccia**, flavored with the delicious regional white wine, and the **zafferano pinolo**, a saffron and pine nut blend that is truly special. The menu changes throughout the year depending on seasonal availability of ingredients, so feel free to go out on a limb while making your choice. Also, be forewarned that there is another gelateria on the square with a tempting outdoor seating area. Do not let your tired feet sway your decision, GELATERIA DI "PIAZZA" is worth it even if you have to kneel while waiting in line.

GELATO LORE

The Gelateria is Born

While the Italian general populace was enjoying flavored ices and sorbets by the seventeenth century, in the rest of Europe these delicacies remained a privilege of the rich. It was a Sicilian fisherman named Francesco Procopio who brought these treats to the rest of the continent. Born near Palermo in 1650, Procopio spent his childhood following in the footsteps of his fishermen father and grandfather, but by the time of his marriage at age twenty-five, he was living in Paris. There he was an established merchant, selling coffee, chocolates, lemonades, liqueurs, and traditional Sicilian flavored ices from three rented stalls on the grounds of the annual Parisian pre-Easter Fair. With earnings from the stalls and other unknown financing, Procopio was able to start a small café of his own in 1675 and by 1686 was successful enough to move to a more favorable location and open up the CAFÈ PROCOPIO on the Rue des Fossés-Saint-Germain (now the Rue de l'Ancienne Comédie). **Procopio's fanciful shop, with hanging mirrors, marble tables, dangling chandeliers**, and house special-ties — including granitas, lemon and orange sorbets, and strawberry sherbet — revolution-ized the scene. This gelateria prototype quickly became the talk of Paris and over time served nearly every famous Frenchman, from Voltaire and Napoleon to Balzac and Victor Hugo. Today, after several ownership changes and a period of inactivity, one can once again visit the CAFÉ PROCOPIO on its original site and taste the desserts that helped make gelato an international indulgence.

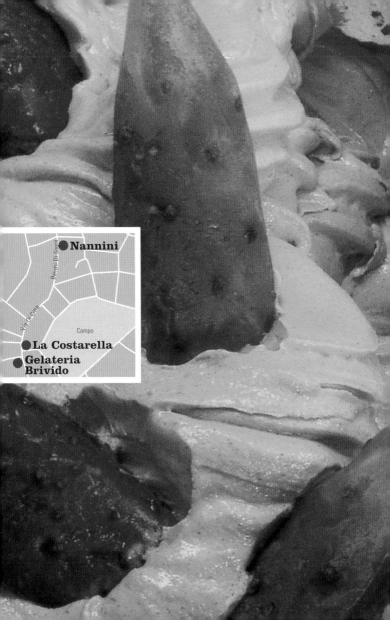

Nannini

Banchi Di Sopra

Via Di Città

Campo

La Costarella

Gelateria
Brivido

SIENA is famous for the age-old rivalry

between the city's seventeen distinct wards, known as the *Contrade*. Twice every summer this rivalry comes to a head at the holding of the *Corsa del Palio*, a medieval horserace on the city's main piazza featuring collisions, sabotage, and the inevitable swarming mob of spectators engulfing the winner. The *Contrade* with the victorious horse (not jockey, because a jockeyless horse can win the race)

celebrates for days and exercises bragging rights throughout the year. Amazingly in this historically divided city, there exists a general agreement as to the town's best gelato, with the following entries firmly established as Siena's favorites. These shops have once again proven the power of gelato by bringing Siena's fractured wards together for a few licks.

La Costarella / Gelateria Brivido

ADDRESS Via di Città 33 / Via dei Pellegrini 1
PHONE 0577 288076 / 0577 280058
HOURS 10a–11p daily
DIRECTIONS *Both are just west of the Campo at the intersection of Via di Città and Via dei Pellegrini.*

Situated catty-corner from each other overlooking Siena's world famous Campo are two of the city's best gelaterias, LA COSTARELLA and GELATERIA BRIVIDO. The shops are owned by the same family, and as far as I can tell serve the same gelato, which leads to the question of why one business would need two gelaterias on the same intersection. The simple answer is that the foot traffic is so heavy and the gelato so good that rather than cutting in to each other's business the two locations have created a gelato nexus and are both necessary to keep up with the constant demand. I prefer LA COSTARELLA only because with its outdoor counter you get a better view of the Campo. Both shops have great **pistacchio** and **fragola**.

Nannini

ADDRESS   Via Banchi di Sopra 24

PHONE   0577 43558

HOURS   Sun 8a–9p, Mon–Sat 7:30a–1a, closed sporadically on Mon

DIRECTIONS   *From northwest corner of the Campo follow Via San Pietro for a block at which point it turns into Via Banchi di Sopra, the shop is located a little ways north on the east side of the street.*

Long before the gourmet market craze hit the States, NANNINI had become Siena's gastronomical epicenter, functioning as a bar, café, deli, bakery, restaurant and, most important, a gelateria. This multi-purpose setup makes the shop a perfect place to watch a Sienese day unfold. In the early morning you can drink side by side with the locals as they enjoy their first of many espressos and eat freshly baked *cornetti* hot from the oven. A little later the tour groups begin to invade, drawn by the neon sea of "n's" and "i's" in the shop's exterior sign. These groups spend a long time perusing the items for sale in the window, which range from the expected — coffee blends and fresh pies — to the unusual — medieval shields, helmets, and lutes. Eventually many come inside to buy treats and mix with the well-dressed Sienese men and women enjoying lunch in the back room. After midday the gelato counter begins to draw a crowd that grows into a mass gathering during the evening *passeggiata* (stroll) period when it seems that the whole town is crammed into the front part of the shop. While all the flavors are delicious, I suggest sticking to the basics here, especially the **cioccolato** and the **crema Buontalenti**, a secret custard-like recipe.

ORVIETO

Orvieto, with its fabulous Duomo, famous white wine, and interesting local crafts, is a perfect daytrip from Rome or a stopover while traveling through Umbria.

Gelateria Pasqualetti

ADDRESS Piazza del Duomo 14 / Corso Cavour 56
PHONE 0763 341034 / 0763 342342
HOURS 8a–11p daily, Duomo shop closed during the winter
DIRECTIONS *The Duomo shop is located on the northern side of this central square.*

The town's charm, beauty, and location draw enough visitors each year that you would expect several gelaterias to be vying for top billing. Instead, competition is nowhere to be found — PASQUALETTI has cornered the market in the city center with two locations within a quarter mile of each other. Anyone who has tasted a sampling of this gelato would agree that its monopoly is justifiably earned. The shop near the Duomo is the place to go, ideally situated in a stone house with an ivy-covered entrance and breathtaking view of the Umbrian countryside. While all of the flavors on the menu, which changes throughout the year according to seasonal availability of ingredients, are delicious, I recommend the **cassata**, which contains candied fruit imported directly from Palermo, and the chocolate-based **Cuban Rum**. The other less picturesque location on the town's main artery serves just as delicious gelato and remains open year-round.

TIPS & INFO

Discovering a Hidden Gem

Speak to anyone who has come back from a trip to Italy and invariably they will rave about some amazing spot they found while wandering off the beaten path. If you listen to enough people you will hear stories about delicious *bruschetta* served at a hill-town *trattoria*, ceramic artisans who create bowls in the same manner as their great-grandfathers, and gelateria owners who handpick ingredients from the surrounding countryside. Be it a restaurant, a merchant, or a gelateria, the key aspect to these memories is the fact that the storytellers found the places on their own. Discovery enhances any travel experience, generating a sense of adventure and fostering a sense of ownership. Acknowledging this, as well as the fact that many readers will be touring smaller towns that are not included in this guide, I have included the following suggestions for finding a hidden gem on your own.

As with any aspect of a trip, **performing some research before you go** will improve your overall experience. Talk with friends who have visited your destination or ask travel agents if they have any suggestions. Internet searches often uncover a gelateria or two and in all probability a shop that takes the time to create a Web site, however basic, also takes time to make good gelato. The advent of the travel blog has opened up a whole new resource for travelers, allowing access to a multitude of first-hand accounts. While many of these blogs are mere ramblings, some are done with care and can lead to worthwhile tips. Once you have reached your destination, the traditional sources, such as information booths and hotel staff members, will often steer you in the right direction.

Nothing, however, can beat **the "follow the cone" method**. Whenever you are walking the streets keep an eye out for people carrying cones. If there is a noticeable trend, such as five people walking by you with gelato in hand within a two-minute span, drop whatever you are doing and follow that trail of cones to the source.

Once you have found a prospective gelateria, the real detective work begins. First and foremost, **check for the all-important *produzione propria*** (produced by proprietor) or ***fatta in casa*** (made in-house) signs hanging in the window. By law a shop cannot hang these signs unless

the gelato was made on the premises. Nearly every shop lacking this notification has purchased their gelato from an off-site producer, which usually means forgettable gelato.

When you first walk into any shop be sure to **check out the color of the gelato**.

Great gelato is most often a tad ugly, so if the gelato is too pretty, then it probably contains artificial flavoring and/or coloring. A good benchmark is banana: if it is yellow, keep walking, if it has a grayish hue, then order away.

The **turnover of flavors** is an important factor as well. Good gelaterias go through several vats of their more popular flavors each day, ensuring a constant supply of fresh gelato. Shops with low turnover often carry gelato that looks like it has melted and then been refrozen, indicating that it has more than likely been sitting around for a few days.

More important, if a shop commits the heinous crime of storing its gelato in plastic rather than **metal containers**, run away and do not look back.

In terms of equipment, most good gelato is **served with an open spoon or spatula**. In the north, I ran into some good shops that used American-style scoops, but in general, a shop serving gelato that hangs off an open spoon is a good bet.

If you are still unsure if a gelateria is worth your time, **ask for some samples** or order a small cone. A sample of bad gelato is not going to kill you and there is never any shame in tossing a cone and continuing your search until you have discovered your own hidden gem.

PERUGIA

Perugia is first and foremost a chocolate town, so it comes as a surprise that a gelateria could maintain a devoted following.

Gelateria Veneta 🏃

ADDRESS   Piazza Italia 20
PHONE   075 5728576
HOURS   8a–1a daily
DIRECTIONS *A short walk south on Corso Vannucci from the Duomo and Piazza della Repubblica, on the northwestern corner of the piazza.*

VENETA, however, is no ordinary gelateria, holding a prized position within both the city center and its citizen's stomachs. From the shop you can either walk south and view the spectacular Umbrian countryside or north and slowly climb into medieval Perugia. I suggest walking from the southern end of Corso Vannucci all the way to the Duomo while stopping for some gelato along the way. On this unusually wide pedestrian thoroughfare surrounded by gothic buildings you can imagine yourself a medieval knight, armed with a cone rather than a sword. When eating gelato in Perugia you must try the **bacio**, named after the famous Perugian chocolate "kiss" (the original and far tastier version than the Hershey's variety). Also delicious is the **cioccolato bianco** (white chocolate) and the **pesca fragola**, which begins with a subtle hint of strawberry and is followed by a refreshing peach aftertaste.

PADUA

Padua is not on the itineraries of most travelers, but it should be a destination for anyone who likes gelato. In addition to the two reviewed shops, GELATERIA SANTAMARIA and GELATERIA MARGHERITA are in a bustling market in the city center.

Pasticceria Lilium al Santo

ADDRESS   Via del Santo 181
PHONE   049 8751107
HOURS   9a–9p, closed Mon
DIRECTIONS   *Just north of the Basilica di San Antonio and Piazza del Santo.*

It has been estimated that five million people a year make the pilgrimage to Padua to visit the Basilica di San Antonio. Casual observation led me to believe that a significant percentage of these visitors are also making a pilgrimage to the nearby PASTICCERIA LILIUM. The shop's window, packed with freshly baked biscotti, cakes, pies, and the famous **dolce del santo** (a sponge cake filled with apricot jam and orange candies), is more than any sweet tooth can handle. I once witnessed an entire Austrian tour group stop dead in their tracks as they passed the enticing display. It is almost as though this is not a shop, rather just a grandmother's kitchen that has been opened to the public. As you would expect from an Italian *nonna*, the care and time put into the homemade gelato make it stand above any other in town. Of the twelve flavors I liked, the **fragola** — with a creamier base than typical fragola — and the **pesca e arancia** (peach and orange) yogurt the best.

Tre Pini

ADDRESS Prato della Valle 52

PHONE 049 6546635

HOURS Fluctuate, closed Mon, December and January

DIRECTIONS *On the east side of the Prato della Valle, near but not next to Santa Giustina (do not be fooled by the gelato stand right across from the church).*

Residents of the town, like their ancient Roman ancestors before them, come to this enormous piazza, the largest in Italy, to take in the public spectacle, shop at the markets (still held on Saturdays), and simply enjoy themselves. TRE PINI (three pines) helps with the latter by providing the best gelato to be found amongst the many gelato shops encircling the piazza. Actually more of a shack than a shop, this stand-alone, nondescript locale would be tough to recognize if not for the hordes of people jockeying for position at the counter, always a good sign for gelato lovers. Of the shop's large selection, I particularly liked the **menta cioccolata** (mint chocolate chip), a flavor common in the States but hard to find in Italy. Also worth noting is the **arancia carote** (orange and carrot), which at other shops usually goes by the acronym **ACE**. Unlike others I have tried, TRE PINI's **arancia carote** does not have the trademark electric orange appearance, but rather is a creamier blend that results in a subtler, more pleasing taste. After getting your cone, take advantage of the piazza's main attraction: lush open lawns, a true rarity in urban Italy.

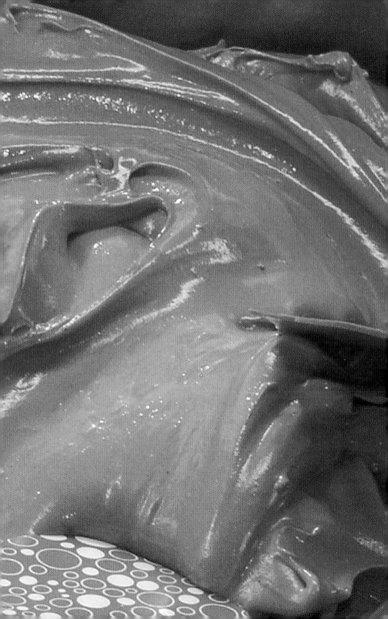

Gelateria Causin

Campo
Santa
Margherita

Rosa Salva
off map

Gelateria Paolin ●

Il Doge ●

Rio Terrà Canal

Campo
Santo
Stephan

Campo
S.Barnaba

S A N   M A R C O

D O R S O D U R O

Ponte
dell'Accademia

Accademia

G R A N D   C A N A L

Fondamenta Alberti

Gelateria Nico ●

Fondamenta Zattere ai Gesuiti

VENICE

For centuries Venice has been a destination for visitors seeking to enrich their souls. The island's beauty has long exceeded imagination and made seasoned explorers feel like giddy, first-time travelers. Today one occasionally hears of people coming back from a trip to Venice disappointed, with complaints ranging from overcrowding and bad food to price gouging and unpleasant odors. As far as I am concerned these visitors should get lost, literally. All you need to become a Venice convert is to stick a map in your back pocket (a necessity for finding your way back) and follow the streets and canals wherever they lead you.

Within minutes you can escape the crowds and find yourself in a bustling market piazza or quiet residential neighborhood. After a little exploration, take time to partake in the Venetian practice of sitting and taking in the scene. Unlike their landlocked counterparts, the island's gelaterias are designed for this purpose, with waiter service allowing you to relax and let the city's splendor work its magic. One note of caution, gelato remains an affordable delicacy for those on a budget, but be prepared to pay up to triple the normal amount if you opt for table service.

Gelateria Causin

ADDRESS Campo Santa Margherita 2996, Dorsoduro

PHONE 041 5236091

HOURS 8a–8p, closed Sun

DIRECTIONS *Northwest of the Ponte dell'Accademia, in the northwest corner of the campo at the end of Calle del Caffettier.*

Founded in 1928, this old-school gelateria does not appear to have changed much over time. Set on a large piazza among fruit vendors, GELATERIA CAUSIN serves a loyal clientele of Venetians taking a break from their daily shopping. The interior has an old, cozy feeling and is a good place to practice your Italian eavesdropping. Outdoor tables face onto the square and are perfect for lounging and writing postcards about the stunning surroundings to friends and family back home. As the vintage signs out front suggest, the house specialties are the **gianduiotto** (see review of GELATERIA NICO) and **cioccolato**.

Gelateria Nico 🪑 ☀ 🐾

ADDRESS Fondamenta Zattere ai Gesuati 922, Dorsoduro
PHONE 041 5225293
HOURS 6a–10p, closed Thu
DIRECTIONS *South of the Ponte dell'Accademia, located between Santa Maria della Visitazione and the Zattere vaporetto stop.*

While the gelato is some of the best in the city, GELATERIA NICO's main draw is its location. The shop's waterside seating area on a pier jutting out onto the Giudecca is the ideal place to relax after a day of weaving through enchanting alleyways and canals. Here you bask in the late afternoon sun and enjoy a cool breeze coming off the open water as you take in the near-panoramic view of the island of Giudecca and San Giorgio Maggiore. If the seating area is full or you do not feel like paying extra for waiter service, it is also possible to order directly from the counter and find your own feet-dangling seats on the quay. The shop is famous for its **gianduiotto**, a Venetian chocolate and hazelnut specialty. The **gianduiotto** has a semi-frozen consistency and is served by submerging a sliced-off portion into a tall glass filled with fresh whipped cream. NICO also makes a wickedly rich **cioccolato** gelato.

Gelateria Paolin 🐾

ADDRESS Campo Santo Stefano 2962A, San Marco
PHONE 041 5225576
HOURS Apr–Oct: 8a–12a daily, Nov–Mar: 8a–8p daily
DIRECTIONS *North of the Ponte dell'Accademia, on the northwestern corner of the campo, across from the church of Santo Stefano.*

GELATERIA PAOLIN is ideally situated on a beautiful square just before the Accademia bridge. The shop first opened its doors in the 1930s and to this day maintains an aura of elegance with its glass façade, red awning, and white-jacketed waiters all inviting you to take a break from sightseeing. More often than not weary travelers succumb to this invitation and choose it as the place to devour delicious gelato while watching the comings and goings of this busy pedestrian intersection. The shop offers a small selection of refined flavors, with standouts including the **nocciola** and the **limone**.

Il Doge

ADDRESS Campo Santa Margherita 3058A, Dorsoduro
PHONE 041 5234607
HOURS 12p–12a daily, closed October
DIRECTIONS *Northwest of the Ponte dell'Accademia, in the southeastern section of the campo, on the corner of Rio Terra Canal.*

Lacking the sophistication of outdoor tables, waiters, and a café bar, IL DOGE seems almost out of place in Venice. Luckily, this lack of elegance does not translate into an inferior product. Operating primarily from a small street-front counter, this shop provides the largest selection of worthwhile gelato on the island. It is also a

great place to take kids, because they can work off their gelato-induced sugar highs by joining the local *ragazzi* in one of the games of soccer that seem to always be playing on this square. Among the many flavors sampled I recommend the **scrak**, almonds mixed in a nocciola base, and the **bacio**, a chocolate and hazelnut blend.

Rosa Salva

ADDRESS   Campo Santi Giovanni e Páolo 6779/6780, Castello
PHONE   041 5227949
HOURS   7a–8p, closed Wed
DIRECTIONS   *North of Piazza San Marco, on the south side of the church of Santi Giovanni e Páolo at the end of Calle Bressana.*

Part café and part gelateria, ROSA SALVA serves some of the best pastries, hot chocolate, and gelato in Venice. Just far enough away from St. Mark's, the shop is able to maintain a local feeling, a true rarity in this tourist-besieged town. Outdoor tables provide the perfect setting for enjoying your cup or cone while gazing at the immense church of Santi Giovanni e Páolo, the beautiful Scuola Grande di San Marco, and the backside of Verrocchio's statue of Bartolomeo Colleoni — a horse's rear never looked so good. I recommend trying the **croccoloso**, similar to cookies and cream but with a nocciola base, or the delicious **noce**. There is also a second location nearer to San Marco at Campo San Luca, though it is more crowded and focused on its popular catering business.

VERONA is a beautiful city. The pleasant

streets, many of which are closed to motorized traffic, world-famous opera, Roman remains, and Shakespearean legacy make it a worthwhile destination throughout the year. In addition to the two entries, the area surrounding the Arena and Piazza Brà is lined with cafés that serve heaping portions of gelato.

Gelateria Caffè Orchidea

ADDRESS Piazza delle Erbe 22
PHONE 045 591512
HOURS 8a–10p, closed Tue
DIRECTIONS *In the Casa Mazzanti on the east side of the piazza.*

Piazza delle Erbe stands over an ancient Roman forum and since the Middle Ages has been the site of an open market. Today it serves as a nexus for travelers, drawn by the beautiful surrounding architecture and an eclectic group of statues that includes two medieval lions and the Fontana di Madonna Verona (which incorporates a Roman statue and looks like a mini-Lady Liberty). GELATERIA CAFFÈ ORCHIDEA is a great place to rest your feet, cool down, and enjoy the hustle and bustle of this most charming of squares. There is a certain satisfaction you get when eating gelato in such an ancient setting — after a few tastes all travel anxiety and mental baggage is forgotten and you are left to enjoy an unforgettable moment. The shop has exceptional fruit flavors including the **tropicale** (tropical fruit) and the **wild strawberry.**

Gelateria Savoia

ADDRESS Via Roma 1/b
PHONE 045 8002211
HOURS 9a–8p, closed Mon
DIRECTIONS *Just west of Piazza Brà, less than a five-minute walk from the Arena.*

GELATERIA SAVOIA proves that not all Veronese love affairs need end in tragedy. Since 1939 the shop has been a favorite of locals and tourists alike, many of whom passionately proclaim the gelato to be the city's finest. The shop has an innovative tradition of creating tasty concoctions that have been copied throughout the world. SAVOIA's first foray into culinary creativity was their **Semifreddo**. This precursor to the ice cream sandwich wedges gelato and Ligurian almonds between two amaretto biscuits. A little later on, SAVOIA introduced the **Gianduiotto**, a hazelnut praline ice cream topped with fresh whipped cream, crushed nuts and dark Swiss chocolate. More recently the shop created the kitsch **Euro bar**, vanilla ice cream on a stick branded with a chocolate € symbol. These creations, plus the standout selection of gelato, have united Verona's citizens in a common cause, Montagues and Capulets be damned. It is worth noting that at the time of publication a bike rental stand was set up just across from the shop, allowing customers to eat some gelato, work it off by cycling through the lovely city center, and return to have another serving.

GLOSSARY

Cestino — literally "little basket," term for the flat-bottomed cones common in Bologna

Cono — cone

Coppa — cup

Fatta in casa — made in-house *(homemade)*

Frullato — a fruit milkshake, similar to a smoothie

Gelataio/Gelatiere — gelato server or artisan

Gianduiotto — a chocolate and hazelnut semifreddo

Granita — nearly frozen crushed ice drinks flavored with various syrups; some versions and almost all coffee renditions are layered between dollops of whipped cream

Gusti — flavors, scoops

Gusto — flavor

Panna/panna montata — whipped cream

Passeggiata — stroll, the term for the pre-evening period when Italians walk the streets and gelaterias bustle

Produzione propria — produced by proprietor (*homemade*)

Semifreddo — literally "semi-frozen," a mixture of gelato and whipped cream, similar to a mousse

Sorbetto — water-ice/Italian ice, typically has more fruit and less water than French sorbet

Specialità — specialty

Spumoni — a molded semifreddo that contains candied fruits and nuts, is flavored with rum, and is served in slices

Tartufo — chunks of rich chocolate and candied sour cherries encased in a ball of chocolate gelato and topped with a mound of whipped cream and chocolate bits

Torta gelata — ice cream cake

FLAVORS

The following is a comprehensive list of flavors
that are commonly available at Italian gelaterias.
While most people tend to stick to the basics,
I suggest tasting a new flavor every once in a while,
you never know what combination of flavors may
please your palate. In addition to the listed flavors,
many gelaterias have unique house specialties that
are named after any number of things including
local heroes, famous artists,
and owners' daughters.
Often these special-
ties use ingredients
that are unique
to a region and
are among the
best choices you
can make. When
in doubt ask the
servers what they
recommend, and/or
taste some samples.

Italian	ENGLISH
Al rhum	*Rum custard*
Albicocca	*Apricot*
Amarena	*Sour cherry*
Amaretto	*Amaretto*
Ananas	*Pineapple*
Arancia	*Orange*
Bacio/Baci Perugina	*Kiss, chocolate with hazelnut pieces*
Banana	*Banana*
Buontalenti	*Fior di panna with a hint of Marsala wine*
Cachi	*Persimmon*
Caffè	*Coffee*
Cannella	*Cinnamon*
Caramello	*Caramel*
Cassata	*Cream based gelato with candied fruit and nuts*
Castagna	*Chestnut*
Champagne	*Champagne*
Ciliegia	*Cherry*
Cioccolato	*Chocolate*
Cioccolato bianco	*White chocolate*
Cioccolato di menta	*Mint chocolate*
Cioccolato scuro	*Bitter chocolate*
Cocco	*Coconut*
Cocomero (anguria)	*Watermelon*
Crema	*Custard (similar to French vanilla)*
Croccatino	*Chocolate crunch*
Dattero	*Date*
Fico d'India	*Prickly pear/Cactus pear*
Fico	*Fig*
Fior di panna	*Pure rich cream and sugar*

continued >>

Italian	ENGLISH
Fior di latte	*Pure rich milk and sugar*
Fragola	*Strawberry*
Fragoline	*Wild strawberries*
Frutti di bosco	*Wild berries*
Gianduia	*Chocolate-hazelnut puree*
Grand Marnier	*Grand Marnier*
Kiwi	*Kiwi*
Lampone	*Raspberry*
Limone	*Lemon*
Macedonia	*Fruit salad*
Mandarino	*Tangerine*
Malaga	*Rum raisin*
Mandorla	*Almond*
Mango	*Mango*
Marron glacé	*Glazed chestnut*
Mela	*Apple*
Mela verde	*Green apple*
Melagrana	*Pomegranate*
Melone	*Melon (usually cantaloupe)*
Menta	*Mint*
Miele	*Honey*
Mirtillo	*Blueberry*
Mora	*Blackberry*
Nocciola	*Hazelnut*
Noce	*Walnut*
Nutella	*Hazelnut spread*
Panera	*Crema and coffee*
Papaia	*Papaya*
Pera	*Pear*
Pesca	*Peach*
Pescanoce	*Nectarine*

Italian	ENGLISH
Pinolo/Pinolata	*Pine nut*
Pistacchio	*Pistachio*
Pompelmo	*Grapefruit*
Prugna	*Plum*
Ricotta	*Ricotta*
Riso	*Rice (similar to rice pudding)*
Stracciatella	*Chocolate chip*
Stracciatella di menta	*Mint chocolate chip*
Tiramisu	*Tiramisu*
Torrone	*Almond nougat*
Tropicale	*Tropical fruit*
Uva	*Grape*
Vaniglia	*Vanilla*
Yogurt	*Yogurt*
Zabaione	*Whipped egg yolks and Marsala wine*
Zafferano	*Saffron*
Zuppa Inglese	*Custard with cake (trifle)*

INDEX BY CITY

BY GELATERIA

Page	Gelateria	City	Page	Gelateria	City
64	Badiani	Florence	34	Gelateria San Crispino	Rome
44	Balilla	Genoa	83	Gelateria Santamaria	Padua
32	Bar San Calisto	Rome	95	Gelateria Savoia	Verona
14	Bilancione	Naples	54	Gelateria Toldo	Milan
71	Caffè Duomo	Pisa	70	Gelateria Veneta	Lucca
58	Caffè Miretti	Turin	82	Gelateria Veneta	Perugia
64	Cavini	Florence	66	Gelateria Vivoli	Florence
19	Commercianti	Bologna	20	Gianni	Bologna
52	Cremeria Buonarroti	Milan	45	Giorgelato	Genoa
35	Da Quinto Gelateria	Rome	35	I Tre Scalini	Rome
32	Doppia Coppia	Rome	91	Il Doge	Venice
15	Fantasia	Naples	76	La Costarella	Siena
59	Fiorio	Turin	46	La Cremeria delle Erbe	Genoa
76	Gelateria Brivido	Siena	16	La Scimmia	Naples
94	Gelateria Caffè Orchidea	Verona	21	La Sorbetteria (Castiglione)	Bologna
65	Gelateria Carabé	Florence	77	Nannini	Siena
88	Gelateria Causin	Venice	36	Palazzo del Freddo	Rome
19	Gelateria delle Moline	Bologna	83	Pasticceria Lilium al Santo	Padua
72	Gelateria di "Piazza" San Gimignano		60	Pepino	Turin
24	Gelateria Ducale	Modena	68	Perché No?	Florence
33	Gelateria Giolitti	Rome	92	Rosa Salva	Venice
52	Gelateria Marghera	Milan	38	San Pancrazio	Rome
83	Gelateria Margherita	Padua	39	Sora Mirella la Grattachecca	Rome
24	Gelateria K2	Modena	28	Sorbetteria degli Esarchi	Ravenna
27	Gelateria la Pilotta	Parma	22	Stephino	Bologna
89	Gelateria Nico	Venice	40	Tazza d'Oro	Rome
71	Gelateria Orso Bianco	Pisa	41	Tony	Rome
90	Gelateria Paolin	Venice	84	Tre Pini	Padua
78	Gelateria Pasqualetti	Orvieto	23	Ugo	Bologna
53	Gelateria Rinomata	Milan	55	Viel	Milan

Look for future
happy belly
guides covering the
shops, shacks and parlors
that your belly craves.

COMING
SUMMER
2004:

happy belly
Ice Cream:
Finding the Best
Ice Cream Parlors
and Custard Stands
in the Midwest

happy belly
Ice Cream:
Finding the Best
Ice Cream Parlors
and Gelaterias on the
West Coast